THE BOONE CONNECTION

IN THE LOST COUNTIES

By:
Debra Webb Rogers

Research by:
Sandra Fender
Debra Webb Rogers

THE BOONE CONNECTION

IN THE LOST COUNTIES

By
Debra Webb Rogers

Research by:
Sandra Fender
Debra Webb Rogers

The Boone Connection in the Lost Counties
Thacker House Enterprises/ June 1998
Copyright©1998 by Debra Webb Rogers
Second Printing 2007

ISBN 978-0-9801919-0-5

No part of this book may be reproduced or transmitted in any form or by any means, electronic or mechanical, including photocopying, recording, or by any information storage and retrieval system without permission in writing from the publisher.

Thacker House Enterprises
Jacksonville, Florida

ACKNOWLEDGMENTS

This book has been at least ten years in the making, and there are many, many people who have helped along the way. I would like to say thank you to the following:

A special thank you to Sandra Fender whose meticulous research and willingness to sort through unindexed records has made much of this book possible.

To my husband Sam, who taught me the computer skills necessary to write this book, and who patiently endured my many trips into North Carolina courthouses and cemeteries.

To my mother, Pauline Webb, who often accompanied me on my many journeys into North Carolina and Tennessee.

To Hazel and Jack Hollifield, who helped me with my mountain research, and opened their hearts and their home to me.

To my uncle Hadley Webb who has always encouraged me in my quest, and who gave me the first clues on where to look.

To the Boone descendants of our Internet group: Carolyn Carpenter, Jim Boone, Donna Trewitt, Anne Friddle-Boone, Sharon Anders, Sherri Wood, Harold Ransom, and Thomas A. Jocobson. I hope I can meet everyone in person someday.

To Jesse Oakes who sent me information that confirmed much of my early research.

To Mary Ina Hampton who gave me permission to use the quotes from *The Descendants of Israel Boone* and *More Descendants of Israel Boone*.

To the librarians and staff at the following libraries: Jacksonville Public Library, Jacksonville, Florida; Davie County Public Library, Mocksville, North Carolina; and Rowan County Public Library, Salisbury, North Carolina.

Deep in the hills and hollers of North Carolina and Tennessee, our pioneer ancestors settled in an almost inaccessible wilderness. The land was steep and unforgiving - and unbelievably beautiful. Some of them deliberately sought to disappear - to escape past debts, racial intolerance, or simply to find more elbow room. Some even came to make moonshine. Whatever their reason, they were successful in surviving and raising families, and in finding such solitude that even today Yancey, Mitchell and Avery counties in North Carolina are known as the lost counties.

Those whose ancestors came from these "lost" areas have found that tracing their heritage is difficult, if not impossible. Many of our independent mountain ancestors wanted little to do with government and society, and because of this, many records, readily available in other parts of the country, simply do not exist here. Finding one's people in the lost counties is often a matter of old family Bible records, tombstone inscriptions, and oral tradition. This is fleshed out, when possible, by census records, deeds, court records and military data.

This book is a collection of many pieces, and hopefully it will solve many family mysteries about those who lived, loved, and died in the lost counties.

CONTENTS

Preface
Introduction

Part One: The Early Boones
    Chapter 1: George Boone.. 1
    Chapter 2: Squire Boone... 5

Part Two: Israel Boone
    Chapter 3: Israel Boone.. 13

Part Three: Jesse Boone & his Descendants
    Chapter 4: Jesse Boone... 19
    Chapter 5: Jonathan Boone... 23
    Chapter 6: Daniel Boone... 25
    Chapter 7: Israel Boone.. 27
    Chapter 8: Sarah Boone Wilson.. 29
    Chapter 9: Anna Boone Coffey.. 31
    Chapter 10: Hannah Boone Coffey... 35
    Chapter 11: Celia Boone Gragg..37
    Chapter 12: Rachel Boone Coffey..39

Part Four: Jonathan Boone & his Descendants
    Chapter 13: Jonathan Boone..43
    Chapter 14: Rachel Boone Wilson..49
    Chapter 15: Jeptha (Jesse?) Boone..51
    Chapter 16: Mary Boone Littlejohn..55
    Chapter 17: Eleanor Boone Clarke..57
    Chapter 18: Jemima Boone Setzer...63
    Chapter 19: John Boone..65
    Chapter 20: Joel M. Boone..71

Part Five: The Mountain Connection

    Chapter 21: Thomas Boone.. 75
    Chapter 22: Thomas Boone Jr.. 79
    Chapter 23: Jeremiah Boone.. 81
    Chapter 24: Israel Boone...107
    Chapter 25: Enos Boone...113
    Chapter 26: Susannah Boone...117
    Chapter 27: Clarissa Boone...123
    Chapter 28: John Boone..127
    Chapter 29: George Washington Boone.. 135
    Chapter 30: Samuel Boone... 139

Chapter 31: James "Big Jim" Boone... 147
Chapter 32: Naomi Boone..159
Chapter 33: Robert Boone...161
Chapter 34: Joseph Boone...169

Conclusion
Bibliography
Index

PREFACE

As far back as I can remember, I heard my father say we were related to the great explorer Daniel Boone. This story was also handed down as a truth in the families of my Webb cousins.

I always pressed him for more information. "How are we related?" I would ask.

He would shrug and say he didn't really know. He remembered that his grandmother's name was Betty Boone. He was not certain who her parents were.

This was in the 1960's, when actor Fess Parker played Daniel Boone in the television series of the same name. I remember watching the program with my father.

Because my parents were always adamant about honesty in our family, I knew if my father said we were related to Daniel Boone then it was the truth - if he had any doubts he would have expressed them.

When I grew older I began to ask for more detail. When I received the same answers I suggested that we try to trace the lineage. I was sure there must be *some* records *somewhere*. My father said he had tried and had decided we would never know - because the people in the mountains "didn't write anything down." He thought there was no way to ever know.

In August of 1957, my father and his two brothers, Jim and Hadley, took a short vacation trip to the mountains in an attempt to learn more about the Boone genealogy. Jim wrote a short account of this trip which concluded with the following:

"So we left Bakersville, the little county seat of Mitchell County. Our search for the missing {Boone} link seemed to have been a failure. However, we had gotten several good leads. It seems pretty definite that Betty Boone's father was James Boone and that they lived around Roan Mountain, Tennessee."

And there the matter rested for many years. I made occasional attempts to learn more about Daniel Boone - reading different histories on his life - but found little genealogical information. My father died in 1970 - without ever learning about the "Boone connection." So it is to him, and to all Boone descendants that I dedicate this volume.

INTRODUCTION

It was almost twenty years later when I decided to take up my father's search for the Boones in earnest.

In 1989 my father's brother James (my beloved Uncle Jimmy) passed away, and at his funeral I was reunited with relatives I hadn't seen in many years. At this gathering an unpublished manuscript circulated called "The Webb Family." It was written by Hazel Webb Hollifield, a cousin unknown to me. (Once I began seriously pursuing genealogical research, I discovered many unknown cousins!) I later purchased the final published volume and realized that it *was* possible to trace ancestors in the mountains - even if the people there "didn't write things down." I began writing to Hazel and visiting her in the mountains whenever I could. She taught me much about the family - as well as how to find genealogical information - written and otherwise. But most importantly, she inspired me with the idea that I *could* solve this family mystery. Without her, this volume would not exist. Thank you, Hazel.

It was in Hazel's book on the Webb family that I uncovered my first clue about our Boone ancestry. Apparently Betty Boone always referred to Daniel Boone as *Uncle* Dan'l. So I concluded that the best place to start my research would be with Daniel Boone's brothers.

But at this point I made the error of skipping over his brother Israel, because I learned he had died at age 30. I thought he probably had few children so I focused on following the more prolific brothers.

It wasn't until I read John Mack Faragher's biography of Daniel Boone that I realized I had been barking up all the wrong trees. Mr. Faragher wrote that Israel's two sons had been raised by Daniel and Rebecca after Israel's death; and that **these two sons had chosen to stay and settle in the North Carolina mountains** when Daniel and his family migrated to Kentucky.

I then began reading the two volumes by Alice Boone: *The Descendants of Israel Boone*, and *More Descendants of Israel Boone*. These I found in the library in Mocksville, North Carolina, and later purchased my own copies. The quotes from these books have been used with the kind permission of Mrs. Mary I. Hampton. (At this writing, these large, detailed volumes are available for purchase from her at this address: 1730 South Delaware Avenue, Springfield, MO 65804). It was in *The Descendants of Israel Boone* that I first found Thomas Boone - my great-great-great-great grandfather - and the lost county connection!

Armed with this information, I sought out census records, tombstone data, military records, placed queries in *Southern Queries Magazine* and on the Internet. I also submitted an article to *The Heritage of the Toe River Valley*. The publication of the Toe River Valley book and the Internet put me in touch with other Boone descendants who kindly shared their research with me, and provided confirmation for much of what I had uncovered.

Family history research is never completed. I hope to hear from more Boone descendants who can add their stories and/or correct any errors in this volume. I can be reached at this address:

Debra Webb Rogers
1840 Thacker Avenue
Jacksonville, Florida 32207

Miscellaneous notes:

- Each person is initially listed with their Boone ancestors in parenthesis numbered by generation - George Boone is always generation 1. For example : (George^1).

- Tables are used to display one generation's children with dates of birth, death and marriage. For dates or names that have not yet been obtained, the cell is left blank so the reader can fill in information that might be found in the future.

- Unless listed otherwise, all photographs are by the author.

PART ONE

THE EARLY BOONES IN AMERICA

"... they did not stay. There was always a branch of the Boone family that did not stay. The Boones were wanderers born. They had the itching foot. Something beyond the mountains always whispered. They heard of distant lands and knew they must go there".
 - John Bakeless, "Daniel Boone, Master of the Wilderness"

Photo previous page:
Interior view of abandoned house in
Lost Cove, North Carolina

Chapter 1

GEORGE BOONE

The first Boone ancestor to arrive in this country was George Boone. He was the son of George Boone and Sarah Uppey. He was born in 1666 at Stoak, England - a village near Exeter. He was a weaver by trade.

He married Mary Milton Maugridge (born in 1669), and they had nine children who lived to adulthood. In 1717, they (and 6 children) left Bradninck in Devonshire and went to Bristol - where they set sail for America. They arrived in Philadelphia on the 10th of October 1717. From there, they settled ten miles northwest of Abingdon and joined the Gwynedd Meeting of Quakers. (In England they were Episcopalians, but after George Fox founded the Quaker sect - Society of Friends - George and Mary Boone joined them. This may have been why they decided to emigrate to America.) The following are excerpts from the records of the Gwynedd Meeting:

GWYNEDD MONTHLY MEETING MINUTES
(1717-1799)

5-26 1720 *"George Boone openly acknowledged in this meeting his forwardness in giving his consent to John Webb to keep Company with his Daughter in order to Marry Contrary to ye Establish'd order amongst us."*

5-26 1720 *"John Webb and Mary Boone declare intentions."*

Marriage record of John and Mary:

7-13 1720 *"Webb, John, of Phila. Co. and Mary Boone, dr. of George, of the same Co. At a public Meeting."*

7-27 1720   *"John Webb's marriage reported orderly."*

7-29 1730   *"John Webb and wife Mary produced acknowledgment for misconduct which is accepted."*

GEORGE BOONE

Children of George Boone and Mary Maugridge			
Name	**Birth**	**Death**	**Marriage**
George Boone IV	July 13, 1690	1753	Deborah Howell
Sarah Boone	Feb. 18, 1691 or 92	Abt 1744	Jacob Stover
Squire Boone	Nov. 25, 1696	1765 NC	Sarah Morgan
Mary Boone	Sept. 23, 1699	1774 Berks Co	John Webb
John Boone*	Jan. 3, 1701	1785 PA	never married
Joseph Boone	April 5, 1704	Jan 30, 1776 Berks Co	Catherine Brown Warren
Benjamin Boone	July 16, 1706	1762	Susanna Likens
James Boone	July 7, 1709	1785 PA	1. Mary Foulke 2. Anne Griffith
Samuel Boone	About 1711	1745 PA	Elizabeth Cassell

* John Boone, a schoolteacher, never married. He passed the family information on to his nephew James, (son of James and Mary), who compiled it into the genealogy that has been passed down.
- All of the above children were born in England.
- All of the above dates are the old-style calendar.

The Boone Connection

Second Generation

Children of John Webb and Mary Boone			
Name	**Birth**	**Death**	**Marriage**
John Webb	1-19 1720		
John Webb	1-14 1721		
George Webb	7-3 1723		
George Webb	7-3 1724		
Joseph Webb	11-6 1726		
Mary Webb	11-26 1728		
Sarah Webb	3-17 1729		
Benjamin Webb	10-28 1732		

Note: John Webb, Mary Boone's husband, was the son of John Webb, born in County Gloucester, England and died in 1711 in Philadelphia, Pennsylvania. His father was Robert Webb - also of County Gloucester, England.

Chapter 2

Second Generation

SQUIRE BOONE

Squire Boone (George[1]) first came to America from England in 1713 with his brother and sister. He was just 18 years old. They had been sent by their father, George Boone, to check out the area to see if the family should relocate there. Apparently the reports were positive, since the entire Boone family moved to America four years later. They settled ten miles northwest of Abington, Pennsylvania, and "joined the Gwynedd Meeting" of Quakers.

In 1720, the meeting approved of the match of Sarah Morgan Boone (daughter of Edward Morgan, an early settler of the Welsh colony of Gwynedd in Berks County) and Squire, and they were wed in September. Six years later, Israel Boone, their second child and first son, was born.

Squire Boone was said to be a man of small stature, with red hair and blue-gray eyes. Sarah Boone was described as a large woman with dark hair and eyes. (I have often wondered what Israel looked like. Did he have the red hair of his father - or the dark hair and eyes of his mother?) Squire was a weaver by trade, as was his father, but he also worked as a farmer.

In 1731, Squire and Sarah Boone moved their family to the Oley vallley on the Schuylkill River in Pennsylvania, where other Boones had settled years before. He purchased 250 acres and built a one-room log cabin. It was in this house that Daniel Boone was born on October 22, 1734. This acreage was several miles south of Squire's father's house, (near the present town of Reading, Pennsylvania), and was surrounded on all sides but one by the homes of three brothers. Three others lived within a few miles. So they lived surrounded by their kinfolk. Daniel Boone later remembered how as a child he spent a great deal of time at the home of uncle John Webb.

Life was not without conflict, however. The records of the Exeter meetings show examples of Boones being reproved for "belligerence" and "self-will."

In the 1740's, conflicts between the Boones and the Exeter meeting of Friends ultimately resulted in the family migrating south. It began in 1742 when Sarah, the eldest daughter, married John Wilcoxen, a worlding, (non-Quaker). It was complicated by the fact that Sarah was found to have been "with child" prior to the marriage. Squire and Sarah Boone stood before their fellow Quakers in meeting and accepted blame, promising to be more careful in the future.

But five years later, Israel too, married a "worldling" (possibly a Native American). But this time, Squire was unwilling to submit to the discipline of the meeting. He even defended his son's right to choose his own bride. Since he was not willing to accept blame, he was soon expelled from the Quakers, although Sarah Morgan Boone continued to be a member in good standing.

They did not, however, move immediately. It wasn't until the beginning of May 1750 that the family began its journey. The family consisted of Squire and Sarah Boone, their eight unmarried children; Israel, his wife and son Jesse (who was born in 1748). Also included were another married son and daughter and their spouses. On a good day they could travel about 15 miles. The approximate route they traveled can be followed by taking U.S. highways 422 and 322 today.

The Boones thus became some of the earliest settlers who left northern settlements during 1750 - 1755 to migrate to North Carolina. This emigration eventually became so large that North Carolina Governor William Tryon wrote in 1766: "...last autumn and spring upwards of 1,000 wagons passed through Salisbury".

The area that became Rowan County was opened to settlement by way of 2 major roads. The Trading Path ran from Fort Henry in Petersburg, Virginia into the Rowan county area where it crossed the Yadkin River at the Trading Ford. It then went on into the Indian areas of South Carolina and Georgia. The other route went from Pennsylvania through Virginia's Shenandoah Valley, and into North Carolina where it joined the Trading Path just east of the Yadkin River.

Land records show that on October 4, 1750, Squire received a Land Warrant and Survey for a 640 acre tract "lying upon Grant's Creek, alias Lickon (Licking) Creek" in present day Davie County (formerly Rowan County). He received a grant for this 640 tract on the present Elisha and Dutchman Creeks on April 30, 1753 and a second grant on Bear Creek on December 29, 1753. An historical marker locates this site (Bear Creek) on Highway 64 West. The Elisha and Dutchman Creek site was deeded to son Squire, Jr. on October 12, 1759, and on the same day the Bear Creek tract was deeded to Daniel and Rebecca. Sometime after the move to North Carolina, most of the Boones became Baptists.

By the end of 1851 at least 812 families lived between the Yadkin and Catawba Rivers. These were divided into three major settlements: the Davidsons - near present day Mooresville; the Irish settlement near present day China Grove; and the Bryan settlement at Shallow Ford on the Yadkin River.

When Rowan County was officially established in 1753 it included the entire northwestern part of current North Carolina. Also in 1753, settlers in the area came under increasing attack by groups of Indians. By 1759 these attacks shifted to the forts and towns. At this point migration into the area halted, and even Squire Boone and his family fled to Georgetown in the District of Columbia. They did return - but not for three years.

Squire died in 1765 at age 69, and Sarah died in 1777 aged 77 years. They are buried in the Jopa cemetery just north of Mocksville on the east side of U.S. highway 601. It is believed that Israel and his wife are also buried there in unmarked graves. It is an incongruous setting -

the peaceful wooded area of the cemetery is located right on busy Highway 601 - right next door to a standard strip shopping area - "The Squire Boone Plaza."

The beautiful Joppa Cemetery in Mocksville. The brick marker of Squire and Sarah Boone is in the foreground.

The Squire Boone Plaza, located next door to Joppa Cemetery in Mocksville, North Carolina

The Children of Squire and Sarah Morgan Boone			
Name	**Birth**	**Death**	**Marriage**
Sarah Boone	June 7, 1724	1815	John Wilcoxson
Israel Boone	May 9, 1726	1756	wife unknown
Samuel Boone	May 20* 1728	1816	Sarah Day
Jonathan Boone	Dec. 6, 1730	1818?	Mary Carter
Elizabeth Boone	Feb. 5, 1732	1825	William Grant
Daniel Boone	Oct. 22* 1734	1820	Rebecca Bryan
Mary Boone	Nov. 3, 1736	1819	William Bryan
George Boone	Jan. 2, 1739	1820	Ann Linville
Edward Boone	Nov. 19, 1740	1780	Martha Bryan
Squire Boone	Oct. 5, 1744	1815	Jane VanCleve
Hannah Boone			

* indicates old-style calendar

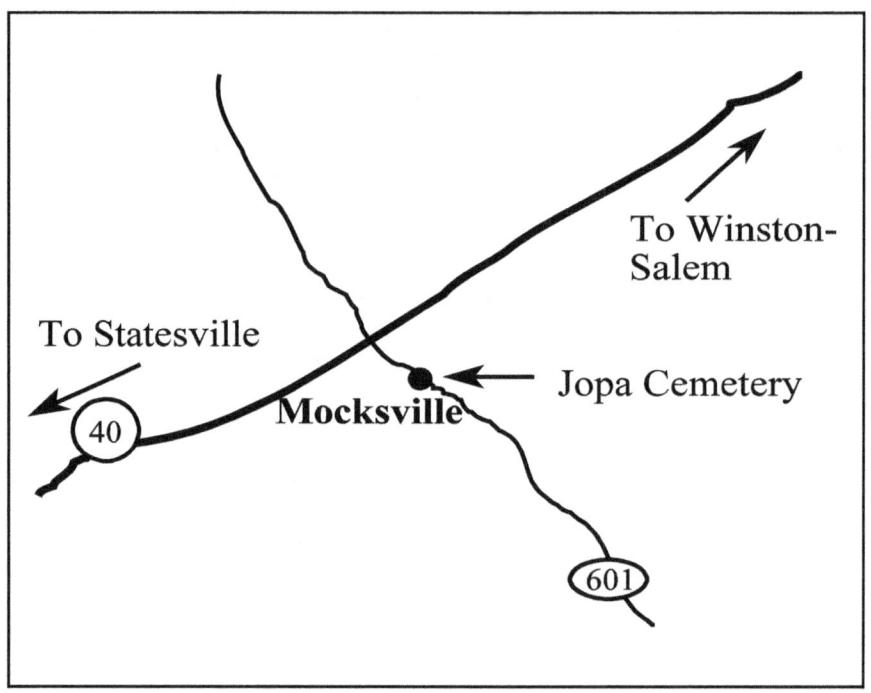

PART TWO

ISRAEL BOONE

"...there being small hope of his recovery".
- Moravian record

Photo previous page:

View of Yadkin River from the former homesite of Squire & Sarah Morgan Boone.

Chapter 3

Third Generation

ISRAEL BOONE
(Daniel Boone's brother)

Israel Boone (Squire[2], George[1])was born in Burks County, Pennsylvania, on May 20, 1726, the second child of Sarah Morgan Boone and Squire Boone. Little detail is known of his life, but Quaker records of December 31,1747 state: "Israel Boone has married out." It is known that his wife was a non-Quaker, but to date I have been unable to locate any record of her name. A record found on Compuserve says her name was Martha, born about 1728, but I have been unable to confirm this. Oral tradition indicates she may have been a Native American. However, Alice Boone states in her book, *The Descendants of Israel Boone*: "...nothing has as yet been found to give credence to the story that Israel's wife was an Indian girl". But this story has persisted and has been handed down in my own family's oral history.

Their first child, Jesse, was born in October of 1748. I wonder what life was like for them during this period. Israel and his wife were denied Quaker membership along with Squire Boone, although Sarah Morgan Boone continued to be a member in good standing. Were they ostracized by all non-family members in the community? Or did living surrounded by their family mean that they had little contact with non-family members anyway?

Whatever the case, when baby Jesse was about a year and a half old, in May 1750, the family began their migration southwestward.

Since Israel's second child Jonathan was born on the 21st of November in 1750, his wife would have been almost 3 months pregnant at the outset of this journey.

After traveling about a month, the family made camp on Linnville Creek, north of Harrisonburg, Virginia, and stayed for at least one growing season. So Jonathan was probably born during their stay in Virginia.

It was not until late in 1751 or early 1752 that Squire and his family actually made the move to the Yadkin valley in North Carolina. (Although Squire had apparently checked out the area in 1750 since he took out a warrant for 640 acres at that time).

As the site for his cabin, Squire chose a hill overlooking the Yadkin River in what is now Davie County. Until the early 1900's the foundation could still be seen. This site is located in Boone's Cave State Park, north of Salisbury, North Carolina. (It is an interesting place to visit, with steps leading down the rocky bluff from the cabin site past Boone's cave to the river).

Soon after settling in the Yadkin Valley, Israel's third child, and first daughter Elizabeth was born on November 28, 1752. And in 1754 youngest daughter Sarah (Sallie) was born.

But soon things began to deteriorate. Not long after little Sallie's birth, Israel's wife came down with consumption (tuberculosis), and died sometime before June 1756, at age 28.

In August of 1755, Sarah Morgan Boone arrived with Israel in Salem, North Carolina at the Moravian colony (located about 20 miles away). She hoped to get treatment for Israel from the resident doctor there. For Israel too had developed tuberculosis. The doctor was Hans Martin Kalberlahn, who had received the best medical training then available, and was said to have been years ahead of his time .

The Moravians kept careful diaries as shown by these excerpts:

"August 26, 1755   A consumptive came with his mother and asked to remain 2 weeks for treatment and we could not refuse."

"September 1.   The consumptive was taken home by his brother, who came for him last evening. He - Mr. Boone - returned on the 6th, accompanied by his father, who remained overnight. On the 15th his brother came for him and he left, there being small hope of his recovery."

Israel Boone died less than a year later, on June 26, 1756.

As to where Israel's children went after their parents death, the records differ. John Mack Faragher states in *Daniel Boone, The Life and Legend of an American Pioneer*, that Jesse and Jonathan both went to live with Daniel and Rebecca.

A letter in the collection of the Davie County Public Library in Mocksville, North Carolina, states that baby Sallie was taken in by Daniel's sister Elizabeth Boone Grant. I would suspect that this Elizabeth may have also taken Israel's daughter Elizabeth, especially since the child may have been her namesake.

A small publication called *Jesse Boone, Son of Israel Boone*, by Dr. J.E. Hodges (also in the Davie County Library), quotes the Draper manuscript as saying that Jesse Boone was raised by Daniel and Rebecca. I have not yet had the opportunity to see the Draper manuscript myself. It may also contain specific information about Jonathan Boone. I hope someday to pursue this.

Alice Boone in *More Descendants of Israel Boone* writes that "no actual clues have been found to indicate which of the relatives raised them" (Jonathan and Elizabeth). She speculates that Jonathan may have been raised by Squire and Sarah Boone. But Daniel and Rebecca were probably living in Squire's household at that time - hence the confusion on specifically who took the children. In *The Boone Family* by Hazel Spraker, their place of residence is called a "double" log cabin, and a photograph of the reproduction cabin near Boone's Cave shows a cabin with two front doors - rather like a duplex of today. It wasn't until about 1764 when Daniel and Rebecca moved to Wilkes County, North Carolina.

Israel Boone

I tend to believe Mr. Faragher's account that both boys were raised in the household of Daniel and Rebecca. I think this explains the reverence with which Jonathan's descendants refer to "Uncle Daniel".

The Children of Israel Boone and his wife			
Name	**Birth**	**Death**	**Marriage**
Jesse Boone+	1748	1830	Sarah McMahan
Jonathan Boone+	Nov 21, 1750	1826	Susannah Nixon
Elizabeth Boone *	Nov 28, 1752	August 1817	John Power, Jr.
Sarah (Sallie) Boone *	1754	1777	John McMahan

* For a detailed accounting of the descendants Elizabeth and Sarah, see *The Descendants of Israel Boone*, and *More Descendants of Israel Boone*, by Alice Boone.

PART THREE

JESSE BOONE AND HIS DESCENDANTS

"... I commit my Soul to God who gave it, and my body to my friends that it may be decently buried..."
— from Jesse Boone's will

The Boone Connection

Photo previous page:
Cemetery of the Zion Hill Baptist Church in McMinn

Chapter 4

Fourth Generation

JESSE BOONE

Jesse Boone (Israel[3], Squire[2], George[1]) was born in October 1748, probably in Pennsylvania. He grew to be between 5'8" and 5'9" tall. In approximately 1772, in Rowan County, North Carolina, he married Sarah McMahan, daughter of James McMahan.

According to notes left by Daniel Boone's son Nathan, "Jesse Boone was raised mainly by Daniel Boone and his wife". Also, Jesse's granddaughter, Mrs. Sarah Henderson said: " His parents dying when Jesse was young, he lived in Daniel Boone's family."

According to the Draper manuscript, Jesse went to Kentucky with Squire Boone (probably Daniel's brother) in 1770 - carrying supplies to Daniel. He was about 22 years old.

He first entered land in Burke County in 1777. He was about 29 years old and had been married about 5 years. He and his wife had one son, Jonathan, at this time, and possibly another son, Daniel. By 1810 he had four tracts on the Mulberry Watershed, in what is now the Boone's Fork Campground.

By 1810, Jesse had moved near Coffey's Gap of the Blue Ridge. The creek that flows through there into the Watauga River is called "Boone's Fork". He remained there until the fall of 1823. Here he and his family joined the Three Forks Baptist Church (more on this church in the chapter on Jonathan Boone). His brother Jonathan also entered land five tracts of land on the Mulberry Watershed between 1779 and 1805. This area has been described as: "...4 miles from Schull's Mills and 2 miles from Kelsey Post Office".

According to the Ashe County (North Carolina) Deed Book M, page 391, Jesse sold his farm of 350 acres on Flanners Fork of the New River to Alexander Elrod for $600. Presumably this was in preparation for the move to Tennessee.

When Jesse and his wife moved to Tennessee, they were accompanied, or joined later, by all three sons, and sons-in-law, Jonathan Wilson and Marvel Coffey. (Three of his daughters, Anna Coffey, Hannah Coffey and Celia Gragg, remained in North Carolina, raised their families, and died there.)

In Tennessee, the family settled on Middle Creek, in McMinn County. There they joined the Zion Hill Baptist Church. Jesse's land grant reads as follows:

"Grant No. 503, State of Tennessee
    "Jesse Boone this day enters as occupant enterer, agreeable to law, the southwest

corner of Section 5, Township 5, Range 1, East of the Meridian, in the county of McMinn, Hiwasse District. Beginning in the Northwest corner of said quarter, 160 acres."
July 27, 1824

Jesse Boone's Will:

"In the name of God Amen, I, Jesse Boon of the county of McMinn and State of Tennessee, of sound and dispositive mind and memory do make and ordain this may last Will and Testament.

1st. I commit my Soul to God who gave it, and my body to my friends that it may be decently buried.

All my property, both real and personal. That may remain after my debts are paid I lend to my beloved wife, Sarh Boon, for her use during her natural life and widowhood. After her death I wish my negro woman, Dinah, be freed and set at liberty.

My land lying on Middle Creek to be divided between my sons Israel and Jonathan according to lines thereto agreed afore,--viz the parts laid off for Israel and Daniel Boone to belong to Israel and the parts laid off for Jonathan Boone and Marvel Coffey to belong to Jonathan, the whole to be valued at seven hundred dollars; out of the property which may them remain I give to the amount of two hundred dollars to Jonathan Wilson, Smith Coffey. William Coffey and William Gragg, which with a negro man named Martin heretofore given to them and valued at five hundred dollars is intended as equivalent to the land already disposed of - then the remainder, if any to be equally divided between Daniel Boon, Israel Boon and Jonathan Boon, Marvel Coffey, Jonathan Wilson, Smith Coffey, William Gragg and William Coffey.

Lastly I appoint Israel Boon and Asbury M. Coffey Executors of this my last will and Testament.

Signed, sealed and published in presence of us this 23rd day of Nov 1829. Witnesses: Jesse Boon, A.M. Coffey Jonathan Allen

Jesse Boone

The Children of Jesse Boone and Sarah McMahan Boone			
Name	**Birth**	**Death**	**Marriage**
Jonathan Boone+	About 1775	1850-1860	_____ Allen?
Daniel Boone+	About 1776-1780	After 1843	1st: cousin Nancy Boone 2nd: Elizabeth
Israel Boone +	Feb 7, 1780 (Burke Co.)	Oct 13, 1839	Elizabeth Moore
Sarah Boone+			Jonathan Wilson
Hannah Boone+	About 1783 (Burke)	After 1860	Smith Coffey
Anna Boone+*	July 26, 1785 (Burke)	Jan 16, 1876	William Coffey**
Celia Boone+	1790 (probably Burke Co.)		William (Buck) Gragg II**
Rachel Boone+	1793 (Burke)		Marvel Coffey

*In several references Anna Boone is listed as a sister of Jesse Boone. But Jesse was born in 1748 and Anna in 1785 - a 37 year age difference.

** William Coffey and William Gragg are listed as serving on the Grand Jury in March 1832 that handed down the Bill of Indictment of Frances (Frankie) Silver. She was the first white woman legally hanged in North Carolina, and the subject of many ballads and legends.

Boone's Fork Trail as it appeared in 1997. This land was once owned by Jesse and/or Jonathan Boone.

Chapter 5

Fifth Generation

JONATHAN BOONE

Jonathan Boone (Jesse[4] Israel[3], Squire[2] George[1]), eldest son of Jesse Boone and Sarah McMahan Boone, was born in Rowan County North Carolina in 1775. He was married in Burke County N.C., but his wife's name is unknown at this time. Her last name may have been Allen.

When he was young he moved with the family to Burke County, where his father entered several tracts of land late in 1776, and in the 1780's. Here he grew up, and in the Burke County census of 1800 is listed with a wife and infant daughter, Sarah Ann.

At some point he moved to Ashe County N.C., either before or at the same time his father Jesse did. The Ashe County deed book states: "On September 15, 1821, Jonathan Boone sold his 245 acre farm on the north side of New River, adjoining the lands of Jesse Council to John Hardin for $600." This land adjoined the Three Forks Church land. This was almost 2 years before his father Jesse sold his land before moving to McMinn County, Tennessee. They are said to have gone at about the same time.

In McMinn County Tennessee, they joined the Zion Hill Baptist Church, and , in March 1834 the church minutes state that Jonathan Boone asked for letters of Dismission from the church for himself and his wife, sons John and Daniel and daughter Elizabeth. This was shortly before they left for Missouri.

Jonathan died between 1850 and 1860 in either Osage County, Missouri, or Maries County - depending on exactly what year he died, since Maries County was formed in 1855.

The Children of Jonathan Boone and Wife			
Name	**Birth**	**Death**	**Marriage**
Sarah Ann Boone	Jan 12, 1800 in NC	Nov 8, 1872	Abram (Abraham) Edmisten
Mary Boone	1801 in NC		Edward ("Neddie") Moss
Jonathan Boone Jr.	Abt 1798 no further info		
Jesse Boone (killed by a team of runaway horses in Polk County, MO)	Oct. 14, 1807 in NC	1876 in MO.	1st: Eliza Anne Cansler 2nd: Julia AnnGelette
Israel Boone	1809		Julia Ann Gelette
John Boone	1813		1st wife died in Tenn, 2nd wife: Minerva Taff
Daniel Boone	1796 or 1816?	1892 in Texas	1st: Judah Helton 2nd: Sarah Jane __
Elizabeth Boone	1815 or 1825?		
Albert Boone	1828		Carolyn ____

Note: There may have been another daughter that married a Grigsby.

Chapter 6

Fifth Generation

DANIEL BOONE

Daniel Boone (Jesse[4] Israel[3], Squire[2] George[1]), was born in North Carolina in 1776 or 1777, and died in Mercer County, Kentucky sometime after 1843.

His first marriage took place on January 1, 1800, to his second cousin, Nancy Boone. They had at least two children, one son and one daughter.

His second marriage, about 1812, was to Elizabeth _____. They also had at least two children, and probably more, but the court records in Wayne County Kentucky are missing the years 1813 - 1831.

Deed records show him in Wayne County Kentucky in 1813, 1829, 1831, 1833 and 1843. But he was also listed in the Zion Hill Baptist Church records in McMinn County Tennessee in 1826 and 1829. He may have moved to Tennessee briefly when his brother Israel and his wife Elizabeth did, since he witnessed the sale of their land on April 23, 1829.

The Children of Daniel Boone and Nancy Boone			
Name	**Birth**	**Death**	**Marriage**
Mary A. (Polly) Boone	Jan 31, 1802 NC		
Daniel Boone	Aft 1802		

25

The Children of Daniel Boone and 2nd Wife Elizabeth ___			
Name	**Birth**	**Death**	**Marriage**
Nancy Boone	Abt 1814	Feb 27, 1834 Wayne Co, KY	Thomas Surrell
Jesse Boone	Abt 1815		

Chapter 7

Fifth Generation

ISRAEL BOONE

Born in Burke County, North Carolina on the 7th of February 1780, Israel Boone (Jesse[4] Israel[3], Squire[2] George[1]), was the third son born to Jesse and Sarah McMahan Boone. He was probably named for his grandfather. Israel married Elizabeth Rebecca Moore (September 23, 1787 - August 13, 1843), the daughter of Daniel and Rachel (Stone) Moore. They were wed on the St. Johns River (Burke County), by Read Hight, Esquire, on October 14, 1802. Israel was 22 years old, and Elizabeth was only 15.

Israel moved his family to Kentucky (Wayne County), sometime between 1810 and 1816. His name can be found often in the court records there, and at least one of his children, Allen, was born there.

In 1824, Israel migrated again - this time back to Tennessee where he entered land in McMinn County. Most likely he was joining his father Jesse who also moved there at about the same time. Many Boone descendants with ancestors from McMinn, and neighboring Tennessee counties can trace their roots to Israel and Elizabeth.

Israel died on October 13, 1839, in McMinn County when he was 59 years old. He and Elizabeth are buried in the Zion Hill Churchyard in McMinn County.

The Children of Israel Boone & Elizabeth Moore			
Name	**Birth**	**Death**	**Marriage**
Deszel? Boone	Dec 17, 1803	Jan 4, 1821	
Nancy Boone	Jan 27, 1804 Burke Co		John Cansler
William Daniel Boone	May 6, 1809 Burke	1878	1st: Emily Triplett 2nd: Susan McAndrew
Rachel Boone	July 29, 1812		David Moss*
Elijah Boone	Sept 1, 1813	Dec 4, 1822	

The Children of Israel Boone & Elizabeth Moore				
Allen Boone	Feb 5, 1816 in Kentucky		
Elizabeth "Betsy" Boone	April 7, 1818 in Kentucky		Hiram Medaris
John Boone	June 4, 1821 Kentucky		Betsy Moore
Sarah Boone	Sept 27, 1823 Kentucky		___ Henderson
Israel "Jack" or "Jake" Boone	Jan 21, 1826		Millie Haigler
Jacob Boone			

* David Moss may be the brother of Neddie Moss.

Chapter 8

Fifth Generation

SARAH BOONE WILSON

Sarah Boone (Jesse[4] Israel[3], Squire[2] George[1]), was born in Burke County, North Carolina. She was probably the first daughter born to Jesse and Sarah.

She married Jonathan Wilson (born about 1780), and they probably moved to McMinn County Tennessee when her parents and other siblings did around 1823 or 1824. Sarah and Jonathan had at least two children.

The Children of Sarah Boone & Jonathan Wilson			
Name	**Birth**	**Death**	**Marriage**
Levi Wilson (became a minister)	Aft. 1800		
Israel Wilson	Aft. 1800		

Chapter 9

Fifth Generation

ANNA BOONE COFFEY

Anna Boone (Jesse[4] Israel[3], Squire[2] George[1]), was born on July 26, 1785 in Burke County, North Carolina. On what was probably a colorful fall day, (October 18, 1804), in a log cabin one mile east of Boone, North Carolina, she became the bride of William Coffey (born November 29, 1782). He was the son of Thomas and Sally (Fields) Coffey. William was the half-brother of Smith Coffey who had married Anna's sister Hannah about two years earlier.

Anna and William had 5 children that I have a record of - four sons and one daughter. She and William apparently lived their entire life in the Mulberry Township of North Carolina. The following is from Anna's obituary from *The Caldwell Messenger*, Thursday, January 20, 1876:

"...old Mrs. Coffey, a near relative of Daniel Boone, and the oldest lady in the county, died at her residence on Mulberry Creek last Sunday morning, aged about 90 years. About five years ago she visited Lenoir, and this was the first time she had been out of her immediate neighborhood".

Anna Boone is buried on the hillside of the Rufus Moore Cemetery in Mulberry Township, Caldwell County, North Carolina.

THE BOONE CONNECTION

The Children of Anna Boone & William Coffey			
Name	**Birth**	**Death**	**Marriage**
Daniel Boone Coffey+	Nov 12, 1805	1862	Clarissa Estes
Wellborn Coffey+	May 14, 1807	Nov 25, 1897	Sarah (Sally) Cottrell
Gilliam Coffey	May 21, 1810		1st: Polly Moore 2nd: Susan Gragg
Celia Coffey	June 29, 1813	1899	Hezekiah Curtis
Calvin Coffey	Sept 30, 1819	April 2, 1847	Mary Greene

Note: In *The Descendants of Israel Boone* is this reference:
  "*Following the above list of names written in the Anna Coffey Bible is written: 'Transcribed on this large Bible this 24th day of August 1831. Whoever sees this please let it remain in the big Bible and oblige --Anna Coffey'.*"

Sixth Generation

Daniel Coffey

Daniel Coffey, (Anna[5], Jesse[4] Israel[3], Squire[2] George[1]) was born on November 12, 1805 and married Clarissa Estes (1817-1854). They had nine children together.
  Daniel died at age 57, in 1862.

The Children of Daniel Coffey & Clarissa Estes			
Name	**Birth**	**Death**	**Marriage**
Emily Coffey	1836		
Drury Coffey	1838		Harriett Collett
Martha E. Coffey	1839		Elijah L. Moore

ANNA BOONE COFFEY

The Children of Daniel Coffey & Clarissa Estes			
Sophronia Coffey	1841		Henry C. Coffey*
Jonah Coffey	1843		
Israel Coffey	1845		
Julia Coffey	1847		
Hezakiah Coffey	1852		
Celia Coffey	1855		

* Henry C. Coffey was the son of McCaleb Coffey and Elizabeth Collett.

Sixth Generation

Wellborn Coffey

Wellborn Coffey (Anna[5], Jesse[4] Israel[3], Squire[2] George[1]), was born May 14, 1807, and married Sarah (Sally) Cottrell. They had nine children together.

Wellborn lived a long life, dying at age 90 on November 25, 1897.

The Children of Wellborn Coffey & Sarah Cottrell Coffey			
Name	Birth	Death	Marriage
William Rufus Coffey	1832	1902	Harriett Moore
Milton Coffey	1834		
Thomas Milton Coffey	1835	1863 Died at Gettysburg	
Mira Coffey	1836		
James Coffey	1839	1863 Died at Gettysburg	
Minerva Jane Coffey	1844	1934	John H. Nelson
J. Calvin Coffey	1848		

The Children of Wellborn Coffey & Sarah Cottrell Coffey			
Finley Patterson Coffey	1848	1947	Mary Elizabeth (Bettie) Tuttle
Charlotte Caroline Coffey	1851	1944	Jesse Richard Moore

Chapter 10

Fifth Generation

HANNAH BOONE COFFEY

Hannah Boone (Jesse[4] Israel[3], Squire[2] George[1]), was born about 1783/85 in Burke County, North Carolina. She married Smith Coffey (born 1776 in Albemarle County, Virginia), the half-brother of her sister Anna's husband William. He was the son of Thomas and Elizabeth (Smith) Coffey, and they moved to Wilkes County, North Carolina soon after William was born. Hannah and William were wed in about 1802, in Burke County, when she was 19 years old, and he was 26. They went on to have at least seven children.

The last time Hannah appears in the census is in 1860 in Caldwell County, North Carolina, so she must have died sometime after that. William preceded her in death, dying in 1841 (also in Caldwell County) - he was only 45 years old.

The Children of Hannah Boone Coffey & Smith Coffey			
Name	**Birth**	**Death**	**Marriage**
Squire Coffey	Abt 1803		1st: Nancy Moore 2nd: Ella Webb
John Morgan Coffey	Abt 1805-1809	Before 1870	Elizabeth Day
Leland Coffey	1806		Myra Day
Sarah (Sallie) Coffey	1807		William Puett
Isaac Coffey	1814		Sallie Estes

The Children of Hannah Boone Coffey & Smith Coffey			
Nathan Coffey	Jan 27, 1820		Polly McGuire
Millie Coffey	Aft 1820		1st: Wiley Standley 2nd: John Tritt
Smith Coffey	1832	Aft. 1914	

Chapter 11

Fifth Generation

CELIA BOONE GRAGG

Celia Boone (Jesse[4] Israel[3], Squire[2] George[1]), was born in 1790, probably in Burke County, North Carolina. She married William (Buck) Gragg II, son of William Gragg I and Elizabeth (Pulliam) Gragg. William II was born Albemarle County, Virginia also in 1790.
Celia died in 1874.

The Children of Celia Boone Gragg & William (Buck) Gragg			
Name	**Birth**	**Death**	**Marriage**
Allen Gragg+	Aft 1810		
John Gragg	Aft 1810		
William Gragg III	1811		Susannah Greene
Isom Gragg	Aft 1812		
Enoch Gragg	Aft 1812		
Jesse Gragg	Aft 1812		1st: ____ Mast 2nd: Margaret LeGrand Webb
America Gragg	Aft 1812		Lewis Harris
Eliza Gragg	April 5, 1836	July 24, 1907	Judson Moore

37

Sixth Generation

Allen Gragg

Allen Gragg (Celia[5], Jesse[4] Israel[3], Squire[2] George[1]), was born in 1807 and married Mary Gilbert (born 1805), in Burke County, North Carolina. They had at least six children together.

Allen died in Buncombe County, North Carolina.

The Children of Allen Gragg & Mary Gilbert Gragg			
Name	**Birth**	**Death**	**Marriage**
John Shelby Gragg	May 26, 1842	Oct.10, 1929	1st: Nancy Jane Burnett 2nd: Sarah Jane Hemphill
Manerva Avaline Gragg	1827		
James Osmond Gragg	1828		
William Alphonso Gragg	1831		
Celia Caroline Gragg	1837		
Luzenia Emaline Gragg	1841		

Chapter 12

Fifth Generation

RACHEL BOONE COFFEY

Rachel Boone (Jesse[4] Israel[3], Squire[2] George[1]), was born in Burke County, around 1793 or 1794. She married Asbury(?) Marvel Coffey on February 2, 1813 when she was about 20 years old. He was born about 1790, making him about 23.

They moved to Wayne County Kentucky - the same place Rachel's brothers Israel and Daniel lived - so they probably moved at about the same time.

When Rachel's father Jesse died in 1829 or 1830, Rachel and her husband lived in Jesse's house, (probably with Jesse's widow Elizabeth) until 1835 when they moved again - this time to Osage County, Missouri. Rachel's brother Jonathan had moved there before them. Once again, the Boone wanderlust is apparent! One possible reason for the move may be indicated by the minutes of the Zion Hill Baptist Church (quoted by Alice Boone in *More Descendants of Israel Boone*):

Page 56, February 1835

"Brother Allen informed the church that Marvel Coffey and wife and Old Sister Boon and Elizabeth Boon are in the habitual practice of evil speaking of each other contrary to the rules of the Gospel, and appoints Brother David Byler and Gideon Cates to and labor with them and report to next meeting".

Page 58, 11 April 1835:

"We the committee appointed at the last Church Meeting at Zion Hill, met according to appointment and after long Examination of the matter got the parties to give each other the right hand of fellowship with Christian forbearance, and get along with each other and not speak evil of each other".

When Rachel and Asbury moved, their family included a two-year-old grandchild whose mother had died - possibly in childbirth, since an infant of this mother had also died. Her husband (father of the two-year-old), moved to Missouri with them. I wonder if these deaths had not occurred, would they have moved at the time Jonathan did? Or would they not have relocated at all?

The Children of Rachel Boone & Asbury Marvel Coffey			
Name	**Birth**	**Death**	**Marriage**
Daughter (name unknown)	Abt 1814	1834/35	William Moss
Lavinia Coffey	Aft 1814		
Elizabeth Coffey			William Patty
Temperance Coffey	Aft 1814		James Orr
William Brazeal Coffey	Aft 1822		
Irvin Coffey	1822/23		
Squire Coffey	May 6, 1818		
Campbell Coffey	1831		

PART FOUR

JONATHAN BOONE AND HIS DESCENDANTS

"... his beautiful flowing penmanship..."
*- Alice Boone in "The Descendants
of Israel Boone"*

Photo previous page:
Three Forks Baptist Church in 1996

Chapter 13

Fourth Generation

JONATHAN BOONE

Jonathan Boone (Israel[3], Squire[2] George[1]), entered this world "on the 21st day of November on the 3rd day of the week, about three o'clock in the afternoon, the year of our Lord 1750", (quoted from the Boone and Power Bible in *The Descendants of Israel Boone*). Little is known of his early life, except that he was orphaned at about age 5 ½. He was raised in the home of relatives, probably Daniel and Rebecca and/or grandparents Squire and Sarah Morgan Boone.

Sometime in 1773, at age 23, he married Susannah Nixon. Susannah was born September 18, 1751. At this writing, I know nothing of Susannah's ancestors. Their first son, Thomas, (who later settled in Yancey County, N.C.), was born November 22, 1774.

It was also during 1773 that Daniel decided to move his family over the mountains to Kentucky. It would be the first attempt to establish an American settlement there. Other neighboring families joined them as well. But nephews Jesse and Jonathan, now grown men, chose to stay behind in North Carolina. Perhaps it is fortunate they did - since Daniel's 16-year-old son James and five other youths were killed in an Indian attack during this attempted settlement. Daniel's family did not permanently migrate there until 1779.

As Daniel's party left for this ill-fated journey, Sarah Morgan Boone, (along with daughter Mary and son-in-law William Bryan), accompanied them on the first half day of the march. As she finally turned back toward home, Boone and his men fired a salute. It was the last time mother and son ever saw each other.

According to *Caldwell County Heritage*, (#64), Jesse Boone entered land in the newly formed Burke County (now Caldwell Co.) in 1777. By 1801 he had four tracts on the Mulberry Watershed, in what is now the Boone Fork Campground. Several accounts say this was an area near Daniel Boone's favorite hunting camp. (Had he taken the boys with him on some hunting expeditions when they were young, and they remembered the area?) Whatever the reason, this was the land Jesse chose as the place to raise his family of eight children. Jonathan Boone also entered five tracts of land on the Mulberry watershed between 1779 and 1805. These lands included much of what is now the Boone Fork Recreation Area in the Mulberry community.

Both Jesse and Jonathan were active in the Yadkin Baptist Church. This church was located on the banks of the Yadkin approximately one mile south of its present location.

According to Caldwell County Heritage, page 213, four marked graves are all that exist there now.

In 1791, the church record states that Jonathan qualified for the office of Deacon. Jesse also served as Deacon at some time. In April 1793, Jonathan Boone was appointed the church clerk, and according to Alice Boone in *More Descendants of Israel Boone*, "the Minutes of the old church Meetings are still preserved in his 'beautiful flowing penmanship'". In 1795, Jonathan was appointed to act as church elder. In June 1796, Jesse was appointed church clerk. In November 1800, both brothers were placed on a committee to assist in building a new meeting house. In April 1810, Jonathan was appointed to "take the Church Book and rectify it". Also according to this account, sometime after 1810 Jesse moved to Wautauga County, and presumably, Jonathan also moved at around the same time - since in May of 1814, Jesse and Jonathan Boone both joined the Three Forks Baptist Church. Later, in 1823, Jesse moved to Tennessee.

Another account (*The Heritage of Wautauga County*, #53) tells of Jonathan and Jess of the Three Forks Baptist Church being reprimanded by the church for excessive drinking. It states that Jonathan was forgiven once, but on the second offense was removed from the church. (This is beginning to sound like a family pattern - Squire Boone and Israel, and now Jonathan being removed from a church!)

Jonathan died at age 76, in November of 1826. Upon his death his estate was auctioned. Some of his possessions included: one rum cock, heifer, one side of leather, one copper still, wagon, one grindstone, sheep, a tar bucket, an anvil, slays, spools, hoe, and hatchet.

Jonathan and Susannah are buried in the Kincaid Cemetery on the old Morganton Road, near Lenoir, North Carolina.

The Three Forks Baptist Church is presently located on Highway 421. It was one of the first churches recorded in North Carolina, constituted November 6, 1790. The original church building stood on the bank of the New River (about ½ mile south from the site of today's church), and was made of logs. During services the early worshipers had to frequently leave the church to warm themselves by a fire built under a nearby tree - since the log building had no windows or chimney.

The Children of Jonathan Boone and Susannah Nixon Boone

Name	Birth	Death	Marriage
Thomas Boone+	Nov 22, 1774	1850- 1860	Elizabeth (Coffey?)
Rachel Boone+	Jan 11,1777	March 10, 1861 or 1869	Jesse Wilson
Jeptha (Jesse?) Boone +	Jan 6, 1779	About 1870	1st: Elizabeth McDonald, 2nd: Mary "Aunt Pop" Odle or Rich
Mary Boone*+	Nov 24, 1780		Thomas Littlejohn
Eleanor Boone+	Aug 8, 1783	March 1820	Jeremiah Clarke
Jemima Boone+	May 21, 1786	Dec 9, 1876	Jacob Setzer
John Boone+	Sept 19, 1789	Nov 22, 1837	Isabella Kincaid
Jeremiah Boone	Feb 8, 1785	Died by Oct 1814. Soldier in the Detached Militia of NC against the Creek Indians.	
Joel Boone+	Jan 19, 1792	Married Martha Patsy Sinclair	

* Mary Boone married Thomas Littlejohn on April 4, 1810. They moved to Rutherford County, North Carolina.

The Boone Connection

Fifth Generation

THOMAS BOONE

Thomas Boone, (Jonathan^4, Israel^3, Squire^2 George^1), and his descendants are listed in Part Five of this book - *The Mountain Connection*. They are listed separately because Thomas Boone is **the** "Boone Connection" for most of us with Boone ancestors in Mitchell, Yancey, and nearby counties.

The Boone Connection

Chapter 14

Fifth Generation

RACHEL BOONE WILSON

Rachel Boone (Jonathan[4], Israel[3], Squire[2] George[1]), was born January 11, 1777, most likely in Rowan County North Carolina.

In approximately 1797, when she was about 20 years old, she married Jesse Wilson (born October 1776 and died May 26, 1860).

According to the 1810 census, they were living in Burke County North Carolina, but by 1820 they are in Wayne County Kentucky along with 7 of their 10 children. Presumably, the other three were grown and married with families of their own.

In 1827 Rachel began keeping a written record of family births and deaths in a small notebook. Since her children were grown at this time, it was either copied from another source or recorded from memory.

In the early 1830s Rachel and her husband and all of their children, both married and single, moved to Owen County, Indiana.

This is the tale of how that notebook was uncovered in recent times:

Martha, the only granddaughter of Rachel's eldest daughter Mary, inherited the small notebook. After the death of Martha and her husband, John C. Robinson, the notebook passed to their son Jesse Robinson. Jesse and his wife never had any children, so upon their death, their household goods were put up for sale. The little notebook was purchased in this sale and ended up being sent to the Boone Family Research Association of Kansas City. Thus, the information on Rachel's descendants was saved from destruction - more than 143 years after Rachel wrote the date - January 1827 - on the first page.

Rachel Boone died at the home of her youngest son Tarlton on the tenth of March in either 1861 or 1869 (illegible date) in Monroe County, Indiana. Her husband Jesse died on the twenty-sixth of May 1860 in Owen County Indiana. He was 84 years old.

The Children of Rachel Boone and Jesse Wilson			
Name	**Birth**	**Death**	**Marriage(s)**
James Wilson	Feb 19, 1798		Jane? Ellen?
Mary Wilson	June 4, 1799	1878	John Cooper
Elizabeth Wilson	May 25, 1800		Capt. William Cooper
John Wilson	Aug 18, 1801		Rebecca Coffey*
Allen Wilson	Dec 7, 1802		Mary A. ____
Abner Wilson	Mar 4, 1804		Hannah Allen
Jonathan Wilson	April 20, 1805		
Susannah Wilson	Jan 3, 1807		Isaac Newland Pirtle
Hannah Wilson	Jan 20, 1809		Hodge R. Coffey
Tarlton Wilson	Sept 24, 1811		Charlotte ____

* Rebecca - daughter of John and Hannah

Chapter 15

Fifth Generation

JEPTHA (JESSE?) BOONE

Jeptha (Jesse?) Boone (Jonathan[4], Israel[3], Squire[2] George[1]), was born in Burke County North Carolina on the 6th of January 1770. He apparently inherited the Boone wanderlust, for he left home at age 21 and went to Kentucky, Tennessee and many other places such as : Elk Spring Creek, Beaver Creek, Harmon Creek, and Wayne County, Kentucky.

He was married twice, first to Elizabeth McDonald, and they had at least nine children, but the names of only two are known at this time. His second marriage was to Mary ("Aunt Pop") Odle or Rich. They had at least three children together, and three others that may have been his or hers or both. "Aunt Pop" was born in January 1816/17 and lived to be 104 years old.

The Children of Jeptha (Jesse?) Boone and Elizabeth McDonald Boone			
Name	Birth	Death	Marriage
Jonathan Boone	1810-1815		
Daniel Asbury Boone	1820-1825		
Census records indicate 7 other children, 5 girls and 2 boys - names unknown.			

Children of either Jeptha or Aunt Pop or both			
Name	**Birth**	**Death**	**Marriage**
Nancy Boone	1835		
Stephen Boone	1838	Killed in Civil War	
John Boone	1840		

JEPTHA (JESSE) BOONE

Children known to be Jeptha and Aunt Pop's			
Name	**Birth**	**Death**	**Marriage**
Louisa Cerealda Boone	1844		
Samuel Boone*	1846	1921	1st: Juda M. Thurman, 2nd: Katherine Thurman, 3rd: Sarah Capps, 4th: Sally Jackson Geralds
George Riley Boone	Oct 28, 1855		

*An extensive list of Samuel's descendants can be found in *More Descendants of Israel Boone*.

The Boone Connection

Chapter 16

Fifth Generation

MARY BOONE LITTLEJOHN

Mary Boone (Jonathan[4], Israel[3], Squire[2] George[1]), was born on November 21, 1780, in Burke County, North Carolina. She married Thomas Littlejohn on April 4, 1810, when she was about 30 years old. Soon after their marriage they moved to Rutherford County, North Carolina, where they raised at least five children. Only two of their names are known.

The Children of Thomas Littlejohn and Mary Boone Littlejohn			
Name	**Birth**	**Death**	**Marriage**
Azor Tillman Littlejohn+	Aug 1812	May 9, 1888	1st: Margaret Boone (1st cousin) 2nd: Elizabeth S. (Bowman) Moody
John Littlejohn	Abt 1822		Sarah A. Boone (1st cousin)
A daughter	Information on these last three children is from the 1820 census.		
A son			
A son			

Sixth Generation

The Boone Connection

Azor Tillman Littlejohn

Azor Tillman Littljohn (Mary[5], Jonathan[4], Israel[3], Squire[2] George[1]), was born in August 1812, probably in Rutherford County, North Carolina, since his parents moved there soon after their marriage. He married his first cousin, Margaret Boone, the daughter of John Boone and Isabella Kincaid. Together they had seven children - one son, John, was killed at Gettysburg in the Civil War, on July 3, 1863. A daughter, Isabelle, lost her husband, Joe Williams in the war as well.

Azor died on May 9, 1888, aged 75 years. He is buried in the Littlejohn Methodist Church Cemetery. Margaret died of tuberculosis when she was 35 years old, on December 30, 1855. She is buried in the Kincaid Cemetery with her parents.

The Children of Azor Littlejohn and Margaret Boone Littlejohn			
Name	**Birth**	**Death**	**Marriage**
John Boone Littlejohn	Abt. 1841	July 3, 1863 (Gettysburg)	Sarah L. Boone (daughter of John & Isabella)
Mary Isabelle Littlejohn	Dec 21, 1839	February 16, 1921	1st: Joe Williams, 2nd: Benjamin Franklin Taylor
Susan Littlejohn	Abt. 1843		
Thomas Littlejohn	Abt. 1846		
Sarah Frances Littlejohn			
W. Shuford Littlejohn *	May 20, 1852	October 17, 1901	Dicy E. Anderson
Martha Littlejohn	1854		

* Shuford Littlejohn and his wife Dicy are buried at Flemings Chapel Baptist Church in Caldwell County, North Carolina. It is near Littlejohn Methodist Church in the old Boone neighborhood.

Chapter 17

Fifth Generation

ELEANOR BOONE CLARKE

Eleanor Boone, (Jonathan[4], Israel[3], Squire[2] George[1]) was born in Burke County, North Carolina on the 8th of August 1783. Her nickname was "Nellie". On February 9, 1804, when she was about 21 years old, she married Jeremiah Clarke. He was born in 1778, and was the son of Alexander Clarke who settled in Burke at about the time it became a county.

The book *Here Will I Dwell* by Nancy Alexander contains this reference:

"In the Clarke Cemetery about a quarter of a mile from the old home place, is a tiny rose bush growing at the foot of Cornelius' mother's (Eleanor's) grave, which was planted over a hundred years ago by a family slave, who was affectionately known as 'Aunt Chainey'."

Eleanor died in March 1820, when she was just 37 years old. Her youngest son was not yet two years old when she died. As mentioned above, she is buried in the Clarke Family Cemetery, near the site of the old Clarke home, in Caldwell County, North Carolina.

The Children of Jeremiah Clarke and Eleanor Boone			
Name	**Birth**	**Death**	**Marriage**
Mornen* Clarke	Jan 4, 1805		Levi Hartley
Jehu Clarke	Sept 27, 1806		
Cornelius Wellington Clarke+	May 23, 1808	Aug 8, 1878	Susan Bogle
Clinton Clarke		died young	unmarried
Nathan Lytle Clarke+	Feb 7, 1812	Sept 12, 1906	1st: Evaline Delia Powell 2nd: Mrs. Emily Puckett
John Hugh Clarke	Dec 23, 1813		Mary Allen

THE BOONE CONNECTION

The Children of Jeremiah Clarke and Eleanor Boone			
Susan Minerva Clarke+	Feb 13, 1816		1st: David Crawford, 2nd: __McIntosh, 3rd: Dr. __ Wilson
Thomas D. Clarke	June 27, 1818		

* According to the "Descendants of Israel Boone" page 47, her brother Nathan's notes spell it "Mourning", but "Mornen" was the spelling in her father's notes.

Sixth Generation

Cornelius Wellington Clarke

Cornelius Wellington Clarke (Eleanor[5], Jonathan[4], Israel[3], Squire[2,] George[1]), was born on May 23, 1808. He married Susan Bogle (born on December 27, 1811), in 1833 and they had eight children.

Cornelius was know as "General Clarke" because he was a general in the Home Guard during the Civil War, because he was too old to go to war.

After the death of John Boone (sheriff), Cornelius took John's son Joel Nixon (then about 13), and raised him to adulthood.

Cornelius died at age 70, on August 5th or 8th ,1878.

The Children of Cornelius Wellington Clarke and Susan Bogle Clarke			
Name	Birth	Death	Marriage(s)
William Boone Clarke**	1834	1906	Emma Powell
Joseph Bogle Clarke***	1837	1910	Eliza Hartley

The Children of Cornelius Wellington Clarke and Susan Bogle Clarke			
Samuel McAffee Clarke ("Mack")	1839	1914	Emma Shell
Robert Burns Clarke*	1841	May 18, 1865	
David Porter Clarke	1844	July 18, 1863	never married - killed at Gettysburg
George Rogers Clarke	June 7, 1847	March 5, 1920	Elizabeth Farthing
Franklin Pierce Clarke	Sept 20, 1850	Dec 27, 1898	Mary Ann Halyburton
Mary Eleanor "Ellen" Clarke	April 1, 1852	July 14, 1889	John R. Steele

*   Robert Burns Clark died in Fort Hamby, on the Yadkin River in Wilkes County, North Carolina.
**   William studied medicine and was a surgeon in the Civil War.
***   Joseph was the first mayor of Blowing Rock, NC.

Sixth Generation

Nathan Lytle Clarke

Nathan Lytle Clarke (Eleanor[5], Jonathan[4], Israel[3], Squire[2] George[1]), was born on February 7, 1812 in Burke County North Carolina. He was married twice, first to Evaline Delia Powell on November 14, 1839. She was the daughter of George Powell and Lucinda Rowe. Nathan and Eveline had nine children together. Nathan's second wife was Emily Puckett.

Nathan was one of the first graduates of Wake Forest College, and was ordained to the ministry in Lower Creek Baptist Church in Lenoir, North Carolina. During his married life he held family worship services at home every morning and evening. He only missed this ritual once - the night his first wife died.

During the war he was a missionary to soldiers in Alabama and Mississippi.

Nathan died on September 12, 1906, in Decatur, Mississippi, aged about 96 years old. Eveline died on September 8, 1859, four days after the birth of her youngest daughter - who was named for her. So I suspect she probably died from complications of childbirth. She was 36 years old.

The Children of Nathan Lytle Clarke and Eveline Delia Powell Clarke			
Name	**Birth**	**Death**	**Marriage**
Andrew Clarke		of TB	Mattie __
Mary Clarke			Richard Williams
George Powell Clarke	March 22, 1844	June 28, 1918	Martha Ann Puckett
John Boone Clarke	Jan 2, 1851	Nov 30, 1912	Harriet Elizabeth Cross
Cyrus Poore Clarke	Nov 21, 1852	Aug 6, 1925	Julia Ann Jordan
Julia Lucinda Clarke		1937/39	Pleasant Terry Williams
Nathan Lytle Clarke, Jr., MD			Carrie Melton
Susan Minerva Clarke+	Feb 13, 1816		Asa Gallaspy
Eveline Delia Clarke	Sept. 4, 1859	Sept 29, 1948	John Isham Parks

The Children of Nathan Lytle Clarke & Emily Puckett			
Name	**Birth**	**Death**	**Marriage**
Lee Murrell Clarke*	Nov 8, 1865	Jan 8, 1940	Frances Della Jones

* Lee was a physician in Pelahatchie, Mississippi.

Eleanor Boone Clarke

Sixth Generation

Susan Minerva Clarke

Susan Minerva Clarke (Eleanor[5], Jonathan[4], Israel[3], Squire[2] George[1]) was born on February 13, 1816, and was married three times. Her first husband was David Crawford, and they lived three miles south of Taylorsville. They had one son, David. Next she married a McIntosh, whose first name is unknown at this writing; and then she married a Dr. Wilson.
Susan died near Charlotte, North Carolina.

The Boone Connection

Chapter 18

Fifth Generation

JEMIMA BOONE SETZER

Jemima Boone (Jonathan[4], Israel[3], Squire[2] George[1]), was born on May 21, 1786 in Burke County, North Carolina. She married Jacob Setzer, son of Adam Setzer.

They had no biological children, but raised a foster child - Isabel Holt. She married John McCall, a miller. One of their sons, Jacob M. McCall, inherited the property of Jacob and Jemima, and took care of them in their declining years.

THE BOONE CONNECTION

Chapter 19

Fifth Generation

JOHN BOONE

John Boone (Jonathan[4], Israel[3], Squire[2] George[1]), was born on September 19, 1789, in Burke County, North Carolina. He was the youngest of Jonathan and Susannah Boone's seven children.

An interesting account on John Boone can be found in *Caldwell County Heritage* (#65). It tells of his daughter, Mary Matilda (known as "Tillie Setzer") because she was raised by her grandfather, Adam Setzer. Her mother, Polly Setzer and John Boone were never married. Mary Matilda was born on January 23, 1817, and died November 28, 1906.

John married Isabella Kincaid on August 27, 1818. She was the daughter of Robert and Margaret (Dunn) Kincaid, and granddaughter of the Scottish immigrant, John Kincaid. Both served in the Revolutionary War.

John Boone was the sheriff of Burke County when Frankie Silver (one of the few women ever hanged in North Carolina) was executed for the murder of her husband. Apparently a kind and compassionate man, John Boone found that having to carry out this duty of his office was almost more than he could stand. Oral tradition says that he was so grief-stricken over the hanging he never quite regained his health. Due to his popularity, he was elected to a second term as sheriff, but was unable to completely carry out his duties. He died while in office on November 22, 1837.

In the 1840 census, Isabella is listed as the head of a household that included six children and seven slaves.

Descendant James M. Kincaid stated in his memoirs that his beloved Uncle John Boone was "without blemish."

John and Isabella are buried in the Kincaid Cemetery, near Lenoir, North Carolina.

The Children of John Boone and Polly Setzer			
Name	Birth	Death	Marriage(s)
Mary Matilda Setzer+	Jan. 23, 1817	Nov 28, 1906	Madison Estes

Sixth Generation

Mary Matilda Setzer

Mary Matilda Setzer (John[5], Jonathan[4], Israel[3], Squire[2] George[1]), the illegitimate daughter of John Boone and Polly Setzer, was born on January 23, 1817.

Mary Matilda married Madison Estes (born December 8, 1817), the son of James Langston Estes and Polly (Mary) Moore. Together they had six children.

Madison died on January 17, 1899, aged 82, and Mary followed seven years later, dying on November 28, 1906, aged 89.

The Children of Mary Matilda Setzer & Madison Estes			
Name	Birth	Death	Marriage
Martha Estes	1837		
Harriet Estes	1839		
Langston Lorenzo Estes	Feb 8, 1844	Sept 11, 1923	Mary J. (Polly) Green
Mary Elizabeth Estes	1847		
John Boone Estes	Feb 13, 1850	Jan 28, 1883	Rachel Moore
Madison Elija Estes	1856	1903	Martitia Emeline Moore

The Children of John Boone and Isabella Kincaid			
Name	**Birth**	**Death**	**Marriage**
Margaret Boone	1820	Dec 30, 1855 (of TB)	Azor Tillman Littlejohn (her first cousin)
Sarah L. Boone+	1822		John Littlejohn (Azor's brother)
Joel Nixon Boone	May 21, 1824	Aug 26 1902	Mary Ann Jopling
Robert Nelson Boone		died young	unmarried
William Waightstall Boone+	July 2, 1828	Mar 19 1876	Harriet Elizabeth Jopling (on March 9, 1856)
Nancy Boone*		Nov 13, 1853	unmarried
Elijah Boone+	Abt 1833		Elizabeth(Kincaid) Warlick**, his cousin

* Nancy Boone died after a lingering illness.
** Elizabeth Kincaid Warlick's first husband was killed in the war.

Sixth Generation

Sarah L. Boone

Sarah Boone (John[5], Jonathan[4], Israel[3], Squire[2] George[1]), the second child of John and Isabella, was born in 1822. She married John Littlejohn, the brother of her sister Margaret's husband Azor Littlejohn. John was a carpenter and county jailor in Lenoir, North Carolina. As was the custom, they lived in the brick, two-story jail - the upstairs contained cells for the prisoners.

John and Sarah had eight children.

The Children of John Littlejohn and Sarah Boone

Name	Birth	Death	Marriage
Thomas Littlejohn*	Abt 1846	died in Civil War	
Nancy Isabella Littlejohn	Abt 1848		
Mary Jane Littlejohn	Abt 1850		
Margaret Emily Littlejohn	Abt 1853		
Daniel W. Littlejohn	Feb 7, 1856	Feb 24, 1857	
Elijah Boone Littlejohn	June 2, 1859	July 5, 1859	
Martha L. Littlejohn	Abt 1861		
Ann E. Littlejohn	Abt 1865		

*Thomas was wounded in the Civil War, returned home, but died there of his wounds.

Sixth Generation

William Waightstall Boone

William Waightstall Boone (John[5], Jonathan[4], Israel[3], Squire[2] George[1]), was born July 2, 1828 in Burke County, North Carolina. On March 9, 1856, in Hickory county Missouri, he married Harriett Elizabeth Jopling.

William traveled to California three times during the Gold Rush days - twice before his marriage and once afterward. A fascinating account of his trip with his bride via covered wagon can be found in *The Descendants of Israel Boone*, pages 559-568.

They lived in California for 15 years before moving back to Missouri in 1871.

William died March 19, 1876 in Missouri and is buried in the small Jopling-Boone Cemetery.

The Children of William Waightstall Boone & Harriett Elizabeth Jopling Boone			
Name	**Birth**	**Death**	**Marriage**
Mary Isabelle Boone	April 9, 1857	May 29, 1937	Rufus Lafayette Moore
John Benjamin Boone	Nov 15, 1858	April 18, 1939	Martha Moore
Ida Virginia (had a twin sister that died at birth)	Oct 17, 1860	Jan 23, 1936	Thomas Gamblin
Bussie Varina Boone	Aug 17, 1864	July 16, 1950	Henry Birtwell Payne
Robert Nelson Boone		died at 14 mo	
William H. Boone	Oct 6, 1866	June 10, 1904	Nellie Coleman
Son		died as infant	
Alfred Joel Boone	May 3, 1871	Nov 13, 1957	Sallie Emaline Hirton

The Children of William Waightstall Boone & Harriett Elizabeth Jopling Boone			
Harriett Eleanor "Nellie" Boone	Sept 9, 1875	July 7, 1954	John Thomas Wilson

Sixth Generation

Elijah M. Boone

Elijah M. Boone (John[5], Jonathan[4], Israel[3], Squire[2] George[1]), was born sometime in the early 1830's. He married his cousin, Elizabeth Kincaid Warlick, whose first husband had been killed in the war. She was born on August 2, 1831.

Together they had at least three children, and lived their whole life on the farm Elizabeth owned at Table Rock, North Carolina. She died on December 2, 1915, and they are both buried at Table Rock.

The Children of Elijah M. Boone & Elizabeth Kincaid			
Name	Birth	Death	Marriage
John Boone	Feb 7, 1868	Dec 15, 1953	never married
Minnie Boone (twin to Ida?)	April 29, 1869?	Nov 15, 1957	never married
Ida Cornelia Boone (twin to Minnie?)	April 19, 1869?	June 16, ??	never married

Chapter 20

Fifth Generation

JOEL M. BOONE

Joel M. Boone (Jonathan[4], Israel[3], Squire[2] George[1]), was born about 1792 in Rowan County, North Carolina. He was the youngest son of Jonathan and Susannah Nixon Boone.

Joel married Martha (Patsy) Sinclair on August 27, 1816, in Bath, Kentucky, when he was about 24 years old, and she was about 21. Martha was born in 1795 in Fayette, Kentucky. She was the daughter of Thomas Sinclair and Eleanor Boone Power. Eleanor was the daughter of Elizabeth Boone (sister of Jesse and Jonathan) who married John Power.

Joel and Martha had at least eight children together.

The Children of Joel M. Boone & Martha Sinclair Boone			
Name	**Birth**	**Death**	**Marriage**
John P. Boone	1819 in Bath, KY		
Unknown Boone (son)	About 1821 in Jackson, Indiana		
Unknown Boone (son)	About 1823 in Jackson, Indiana		
Melinda Boone	1825, in Jackson, IN		
Emily Boone	1828, in Jackson, IN		
Amos Boone	1830, in Addison Twp, Shelby, ID		
Mary Boone	1830 same as above, ID		
Martha A. Boone	1836 same, as above, ID		

Old wagon in Cades Cove, Tennessee. The Boones probably traveled in similar ones.

PART FIVE

THE MOUNTAIN CONNECTION

THOMAS BOONE AND HIS DESCENDANTS

Chapter 21

Fifth Generation

THOMAS BOONE

Thomas Boone is the ancestor of all (or most) of the Boones in Yancey, Mitchell and nearby counties. *He is the connection for those of us who always heard we were related to Daniel Boone.*

Thomas Boone (Jonathan[4], Israel[3], Squire[2], George[1]), was born in Rowan County, North Carolina on November 22, 1774. He died in Burnsville, North Carolina sometime between 1850 (when he appears on the Yancey County census) and 1860 (when he is not listed on the census).

Thomas Boone is something of a mystery, since little seems to be known about him, except that he had a large family. He married Elizabeth (last name unknown) sometime before 1800. I know her name was Elizabeth since it was given on her son Samuel's marriage record. The only clue to her maiden name comes from a resident who lives near the Plum Branch cemetery who referred to her as a "Coffey woman". This would make sense since several Boones did marry into the Coffey family. However, I have not, as yet, been able to find any Elizabeth of the correct age in my records on the Coffey family. It is possible of course, that Coffey was not her maiden name.

The first time Thomas and his wife are found on the census is in 1800 (Burke County), each listed as being between 16-26 years old. I do not know where they are buried, although it may be in or near Burnsville, North Carolina. I located a grandson of his, Jeremiah Sullins Boone and wife Mary, buried in the McIntosh Cemetery near the Terrell House Inn in Burnsville. Perhaps Thomas is there too, in an unmarked grave, since several nearby graves are marked only with fieldstones.

It was probably sometime in the late 1790's when Thomas Boone moved deep into the mountains of the lost counties of North Carolina. The earliest land entries for this area were filed under the Colonial Act of 1778. This act served to open the area for white settlement. However, much of this area went to speculators who probably did not intend to live there. Toward the end of the century enormous amounts of land were sold - one entry in 1796 was for 320,640 acres! The price per acre: 5¢.

In the petition of 1825, when residents of Burke and Buncombe County sought to form a new county - (Yancey), the name Thos. Boon appears on the first page. There is also a T. Boon on page 3 of the same petition.

The following is from the marker at the foot of the Burns statue in Burnsville (Yancey County) North Carolina as it appears today:

"On March 6, 1834, John "Yellow-Jacket John" Bailey conveyed 100 acres, including this square, to Commissioners appointed by The North Carolina General Assembly to establish a town site for Yancey County"

There is quite a bit of confusion regarding Thomas' children. At this writing, I have a list of at least 13, and possibly several more that could belong to him. His daughters Susanna and Clarissa each had several children that were listed on census records as living in his household, which only adds to the confusion. I hope some descendant who reads this account will help clear up the mysteries of Thomas' children!

Also according to census records, in 1850 (enumerated October 21, 1850), Thomas is shown living in the household of his son Jeremiah, in Burnsville, NC. The Caldwell County census of the same year (enumerated earlier, July 22 - August 7, 1850), lists Thomas (age 76), as living in the household of his son Samuel. So perhaps during his declining years, Thomas lived with, or at least visited, several of his children. It also presents the possibility that if he often paid extended visits to his children, he may have died in Caldwell County and might be buried there.

These are the children that are presumed to be Thomas and Elizabeth's. Those who may be Clarissa's or Susannah's or a child of one of Thomas' sons (most particularly Jeremiah or Thomas Jr.) are marked by *.

Thomas Boone

The Children of Thomas Boone and Elizabeth Boone			
Name	Birth	Death	Marriage
Jeremiah Boone+	1802		1st: Sally McMahan 2nd: Margaret McMahan
Israel Boone+	Feb 1, 1804		
Enos "Knock" "Enoch" Boone+	Abt 1804		Jemima
Susannah Boone+	Abt 1800-1805		never married?
Clarissa Boone+	1810	After 1880	never married?
John "Johnny" Boone+	1812		Sarah Wilson
Robert Boone+	1814	died young?	
George "Noah" Washington Boone+	1815		Elizabeth ____
Samuel Boone+	1816 in Tenn		Polly ____
Thomas Boone Jr.+	1810? 1817?		
James Boone*+	1824	May 1, 1862	Ollie Howell
Naomi Boone*+	1823 - 1825		never married?
Robert Boone*+	June 27 1823	March 15, 1907	Naomi Howell
Joseph Boone*+	About 1822 - 1832		Delilah Howell

Note: Joseph and Robert are brothers, so wherever they fit, they go together.

Chapter 22

Sixth Generation

THOMAS BOONE JR.

Thomas Jr, (Thomas[5],Jonathan[4], Israel[3], Squire[2] George[1]) was born sometime between 1800 and 1820. One record in *The Heritage of the Toe River Valley*, Vol. II, #235, lists his birthdate as 1817. He is listed on the deed record as follows (so I know he lived into adulthood):

Deed Records, Yancey County, Abstracts, Deed Book 1,
Nov 8, 1838 , 314

*"Thomas Boone Sr. of Yancey County to Jonathan Boon...$100...beg on E. side of N. Toe River runing down said river to branch...up branch to line made between **Thos. Boon Jr.** & James Howell Sr....w/sd line to Branch...down branch to river...down River to beg...50 acres...8 Nov ...in pres of Wm B. Westall, Jurat."*

There is a Thomas Boone (1810-1895) buried in the Brittain Presbyterian Church Cemetery (located on US 64, about 7-10 miles north of Rutherfordton, NC, in the Westminster Community). This cemetery has an historical marker stating that the church was the first organized one in Rutherford County. Next to him is "Margaret Clement Boone (1812-1880) Wife of Thomas Boone". Next to their markers is one that reads: "Susannah M. Boone, August 11, 1846, age 2 months, six days".

Is this the Thomas Boone Jr. that is the son of Thomas and Elizabeth? Thomas Sr.'s sister Mary Boone Littlejohn and her husband Thomas lived in Rutherfordton - so perhaps Thomas Jr. moved there to be near his aunt and uncle.

Census records for Rutherford County show:

1850 - Thomas Boone, age 35
    Margaret, age 48
1860 - Thomas Boone, age 51
    Margaret, 52
    Mary Early, 72
    Matilda, 52
    Elizabeth, 38
    J.G. (Male), 35
    William, 7

Thomas married Margaret Clements on March 16, 1840, according to Rutherford County marriage records, which lists Cornelius Clements as bondsman.

A week after their 12th weddings anniversary, Thomas enlisted in North Carolina Troops, Company G, 50th Regiment in Burke County. He was reported absent without leave in July, 1862. He was reported on duty as a butcher in December 1862. He was hospitalized in Wilmington on August 1863 with anemia, but returned to duty on September 4, 1863. He was then reported absent on sick furlough from September 18 - December 31, 1863. He was finally discharged on February 15, 1864, by reason of "large inguinal hernia, chronic rheumatism, and old age". Discharge certificate lists age as 61.

Children of Thomas Boone and Margaret Clements Boone			
Name	**Birth**	**Death**	**Marriage**
Rachel Elizabeth Boone	1839		
Andrew Boone*	1842		

* Andrew Boone served as a private in North Carolina Troops, Co. G, 50th Regiment - the same unit his father served in. He was a farmer prior to enlisting in Rutherford County at age 19 on March 24, 1862 - the same day his father enlisted. He was reported present in June-July and November-December 1862. He was hospitalized in Wilmington on September 26, 1863, with intermittent fever, but returned to duty on October 5, 1863. Reported present in October-December 1863, and furloughed on February 17, 1864. He was admitted to hospital at Greensboro on March 19, 1865, but did manage to survive the war.

Chapter 23

Sixth Generation

JEREMIAH BOONE

Jeremiah Boone (Thomas[5], Jonathan[4], Israel[3], Squire[2] George[1]) one of the eldest sons of Thomas and Elizabeth Boone was born in 1802 in Burke County, North Carolina. He was one of the first purchasers of a town lot in the newly formed Burnsville's "Publick Square". He bought the lot for his blacksmith shop. These lots were laid out in 1834 and auctioned by the town Commissioners to raise money for public buildings and operations.

Yancey County Deed Book #1, page 144:

Sept 1836   Lot #24 in the town of Burnsville, being to lot where Jeremiah Boone's blacksmith shop is situated sold by the sheriff to Samuel Austin for debt of $35.00.

In 1846, Jeremiah is listed under businesses to be taxed as having a "tavern".

He was married at least twice, and possibly three times - all to McMahans. His first wife may have been Mary McMahan, but I have no further records on this possibility. His marriage to Margaret McMahan, produced nine children, but the names of only three are known for certain: Robert, born around 1836, and Caroline and Margaret, birth dates uncertain. I wonder if wife Margaret may have died in childbirth, and the baby was named for her. James E. is probably one of the children. Also, since only these few children are known, I wonder if some or all of the last four children I have listed as Thomas and Elizabeth's might belong to Jeremiah.

Jeremiah's last wife was Sally McMahan, and their first child Thomas Wesley was born in 1840. So first wife Margaret must have died sometime between 1836 and 1840. Jeremiah and Sally had at least 10 children, and several of their sons served in the Civil War.

According to the following record Jeremiah died sometime around 1885 in Burnsville, North Carolina.

A letter from J.W. Higgins to J. W. Garland dated 2/8/1885 reads as follows: *"I suppose you have heard of the death of Amos Ray and Jerey Boon."*

JEREMIAH BOONE

The Children of Jeremiah Boone and Margaret McMahan			
Name	**Birth**	**Death**	**Marriage**
?Caroline Boone*	1827		
James E. Boone	Abt. 1831		Elendor/Nelly McMahan
Emily E. Boone	1832		Riley A. McMahan
Robert P. Boone	Abt. 1836		Tempie Ann Harris
Margaret Boone	Abt. 1837		Albert Ray

*This Caroline is found on the 1880 census, a widow (did she go back to her maiden name - or marry a Boone?)who lives in the household of her son-in-law, John Melton. She is listed with children Mary (born 1856), John (born 1864), and James (born 1865). Is this the right Caroline?

The Children of Jeremiah Boone and Sally McMahan			
Name	Birth	Death	Marriage
Thomas Wesley Boone+	1840 in Burnsville NC	1919 Texas	1st: Louisia (Harris) Quzsts 2nd: Mrs. Sophia (Armstrong) Sims
Baachus Boone+	1842 NC	Mar 1, 1864	never married?
Sarah Ann Boone*+	1843 NC	Abt. 1901	never married? but had 2 children

The Children of Jeremiah Boone and Sally McMahan			
McDaniel S. Boone+	1845 NC		Saphronia (daughter of George W. & Eliz. Boone)
Edward A. Boone+	1846 NC	1904 NC	Rebecca Florence McCallister
Mary Jane Boone +	1847 NC	Abt 1935	John Ramsey
Lucretia Boone+	1849 NC	1919	Henry Buckner
Mary J. Boone+	1851		
Edmund Boone	1855		
Jeremiah Sullins Boone+	Sept 20, 1854 Burnsville	Apr 24, 1932 Burnsville	1st: Emily Ray, 2nd: Mary McIntosh
Cornelius Boone	1857		
Ennis Clark "Dove" Boone**	March 15, 1858 NC	April 25, 1939 Texas	Mary Lou Tom
Doctor Crumley Boone	1859 NC	July 26, 1933	1st: Elizabeth Cole and 2nd: Suda M. Hemphill

* A record from Family Tree Maker CD # 2 lists Sarah A. Boone as marrying James P. Swofford in 1867. They are listed as having 3 children, John Henry, Elander and Zipporah. Sarah A. is listed as being buried in North Cove, North Carolina, in the North Cove Baptist Cemetery. I was unable to contact the contributor of this information for confirmation. Information from the death certificate of Sarah Ann Swofford: widow of James Swofford, born 1845, age 84 died October 16, 1929. Buried at North Cove Cemetery in McDowell County, North Carolina. Father unknown. Mother Nellie Boone born in Yancey County. Informant was Mrs. T.E. Hefiner. This would seem to make this Sarah the daughter of James E. Boone and Nelly McMahan - or this Nelly is another person entirely?

** In "The Descendants of Israel Boone", Ennis "Dove" is listed as a child of Jeremiahs. But on the 1880 census, Ennis Clarke "Dove" is listed as a *grandson* of "Jerry Boon". He is probably the child of Sarah Ann.

Interior of old blacksmith shop in Cades Cove, Tennessee.

Seventh Generation

James E. Boone

James E. Boone (Jeremiah[6], Thomas[5], Jonathan[4], Israel[3], Squire[2] George[1]), is probably the son of Jeremiah and Margaret, since they had 9 children and only 3 are known for certain. Also, his date of birth seems to fit - plus a probate record seems to confirm it.

The 1850 census lists him as an ironsmith in Burnsville, North Carolina - perhaps he learned the trade from his father who was a blacksmith in Burnsville.   In about 1849, in Yancey County, NC, he married Elendor/Nellie McMahan. She was born about 1829 in Burke County, NC, the daughter of _____ McMahan and Mary(?) McMahan. She died young (20's - 30's), before 1860 in Yancey County.

James E. Boone is listed as a private in NC Troops, Co. C, 16th Regiment. He resided in Yancey County where he enlisted at age 33 on May 1, 1861. He was present of accounted for until he died on November 10, 1862. Place and cause of death not reported.

Records of the Probate Court on May 20, 1870, show Jeremiah Boone as adminstrator of James Boone's estate. Jeremiah states under oath that the deceased was a soldier in the Confederate Army. He was attempting to get his son's back pay for the use of James' wife and children. (Also around this time, Jeremiah was the administrator of James (Big Jim) Boone's estate).

The Children of James E. Boone and Elendor/Nellie McMahan			
Name	**Birth**	**Death**	**Marriage**
Mary E. Boone+	Abt. 1850		Alexander Huskins
Martha A. Boone+	Feb. 24, 1852	March 3, 1915	Greenberry Hughes
Robert Nelson Boone+	Dec. 25, 1852	June 10, 1927	Altha Jane McMahan
Trissie Malissa Boone+	April 1855	July 14, 1933	Tillman Boone

Eighth Generation

Mary E. Boone

Mary E. Boone (James E.[7], Jeremiah[6], Thomas[5], Jonathan[4], Israel[3], Squire[2] George[1]), was born about 1850 in Yancey County, North Carolina. She is listed on the 1850 census, age 3 months, living with her parents.

In 1872, on February 18th she became the bride of Alexander Huskins. Her marriage record lists her parents as James and Nelly Boon.

The Children of Mary E. Boone and Alexander Huskins			
Name	**Birth**	**Death**	**Marriage**
Cleve Huskins			
Rob Huskins			
Alvin Huskins			
Ebbin Huskins			
Twin daughters			

Eighth Generation

Martha A. Boone

Martha A. Boone (James E.[7], Jeremiah[6], Thomas[5], Jonathan[4], Israel[3], Squire[2] George[1]), was born in the winter on February 24, 1852. She was apparently raised in the home of her grandmother, Mary McMahan (according to census records). She was the mother of one illegitimate child, James M. Boone, whose father was Tillman Boone. This same Tillman Boone later married Martha's sister Trissie (Teresa?). When that happened, Martha gave James M. to Tillman and Trissie to raise.

On February 21st of 1875, two days before her 23rd birthday, she married Greenberry Hughes (son of William Hughes and Mary Ann Laws).

According to her death certificate, Martha died of "pnewmonia fever" on March 3, 1915. She was 63 years old.

The Children of Martha A. Boone and Greenberry Hughes			
Name	**Birth**	**Death**	**Marriage**
Mary S. Hughes			
David N. Hughes			
Samuel Hughes	March 1878		
Maggie Hughes	Jan 1882		
Sarah J. Hughes			
Sarena Hughes	March 1886		
Louisa Hughes	Feb 1887		
William Hughes	June 1888		
Robert Hughes	May 1892		
Zebulon Hughes	Jan 1894		

THE BOONE CONNECTION

Eighth Generation

Robert Nelson Boone

Robert Nelson Boone(James E.[7], Jeremiah[6], Thomas[5], Jonathan[4], Israel[3], Squire[2] George[1]), was born on Christmas day, December 25, 1852, in Yancey County, North Carolina. He was a merchant in Burnsville, North Carolina.

He married Altha Jane McMahan (daughter of Jackson McMahan and Barbara Blalock), on January 12, 1876 in Yancey County. Altha was born on May 11, 1861, also in Yancey County They had at least ten children together.

According to family stories, Robert was about 6 feet 4 inches tall, and his wife was about 4 foot 9 inches! She was of Irish descent, and was said to have had an Irish temper. She apparently gave him frequent tongue lashings, and he would just stare meekly down at her. They must have made an interesting pair.

Robert died at age 75 in 1927 of stomach cancer, and Altha died January 14, 1934. They are buried in the Phipps Creek Cemetery.

The Children of Robert Nelson Boone and Altha McMahan			
Name	**Birth**	**Death**	**Marriage**
James A. Boone	1877		Hettie Penland
Barbara Ellen Boone+	April 11, 1878	June 30, 1965	never married
Willard Kelse Boone+	Jan 2, 1879	Oct 25, 1965	Mary Boone
Sarah Ann Boone+	Jan 23, 1886	July 3, 1970	never married
Andrew Jackson Boone			
Mary Martha Malissa Boone+	Jan 16, 1888	May 1980	Ebbin E. Huskins
Woodard Boone			
Douglas Lorenzo Boone	April 4, 1891	Sept 4, 1966	Ester Melton
Carrie Idella Boone+	1896		_____ Rountree

JEREMIAH BOONE

The Children of Robert Nelson Boone and Altha McMahan			
Jeremiah Boone+	1894	June 14, 1918	never married
Jeter Nathan Boone	Oct 10, 1896	May 12, 1921, typhoid	

Jeter Nathan Boone

Ninth Generation

Mary Martha Malissa Boone

Mary Martha Malissa Boone (Robert Nelson[8], James E.[7], Jeremiah[6], Thomas[5], Jonathan[4], Israel[3], Squire[2] George[1]), was born on January 16, 1888. She married Ebbin E. Huskins, her first cousin. Ebbin was born about March 1882. They had only one child, Thelma Elizabeth. Ebbin died of typhoid fever at Fort Leavenworth, Kansas in March 1909, when Thelma was only about 3 months old.

Martha (as she was called), married again in about 1913 to William Garfield Ball, and they had four children. William was a widower (former wife Essie ____), who had a son, Arthur, born about 1910.

Children of Mary Martha Malissa Boone & Ebbin E. Huskins			
Name	Birth	Death	Marriage
Thelma Elizabeth Huskins	Dec 23, 1908	June 17 1985	

The Children of Mary Martha Malissa Boone & William Garfield Ball			
Name	Birth	Death	Marriage
Essie Ball			
William Ball			
Jane Ball			
Benjamin Ball			

Ninth Generation

Barbara Ellen Boone
& Sarah Ann Boone

Sisters Barbara Ellen and Sarah Ann Boone (Robert Nelson[8], James E.[7], Jeremiah[6], Thomas[5], Jonathan[4], Israel[3], Squire[2] George[1]), never married and lived in their parent's home on Phipps Creek. Barbara Ellen was known as "Aunt Sissie", and Sarah Ann as "Aunt Annie".

Ninth Generation

Jeremiah Boone

Jeremiah Boone (Robert Nelson[8], James E.[7], Jeremiah[6], Thomas[5], Jonathan[4], Israel[3], Squire[2] George[1]), was born in 1894, and died under violent circumstances. It seems that Jeremiah never married, but had a daughter (name unknown). Her mother was married to another man, and this man killed Jeremiah for carrying on with his wife. According to a descendant, Jeremiah was another very big Boone, and "rather good looking".

Jeremiah Boone, son of Robert Nelson Boone

(*Photos of Jeremiah and Jeter Boone courtesy of of C. Carpenter*)

Ninth Generation

Willard Kelse Boone

Willard Kelse Boone (Robert Nelson[8], James E.[7], Jeremiah[6], Thomas[5], Jonathan[4], Israel[3], Squire[2], George[1]), was another "huge" Boone. He stood about 6'4" tall, and apparently went by "Kelse".

Ninth Generation

Carrie Idella Boone

Carrie Idella Boone (Robert Nelson[8], James E.[7], Jeremiah[6], Thomas[5], Jonathan[4], Israel[3], Squire[2], George[1]), was born about 1896, and married a Rountree (first name unknown). They lived in Washington, D.C. and Carrie probably died there. They had two sons, names unknown. The following is a story about Carrie from her great-niece Carolyn Carpenter:

"There is a funny story about Aunt Carrie. She was 12 years older than my mother (Thelma Elizabeth), who was living with her grandparents (Robert Nelson and Altha Jane). Once a young man came to call on Carrie, having been invited to Sunday dinner. He was dressed in his Sunday best, and he and Carrie were sitting on a window seat. My mother was spying on them. The young man reached around to scratch his back, and horror of horrors, he discovered his shirt was untucked. He surreptitiously tucked it back in - only it wasn't his shirt he had felt, it was the window curtain. When he got up to walk away from the window, the curtain came crashing down. He was mortified, and that was the last Carrie ever say of that young man".

Headstone of Trissie and Tillman in Plum Branch Cemetery, NC.

Eighth Generation

Trissie Malissa Boone and Tillman Boone

Trissie Malissa Boone, (James E.[7], Jeremiah[6], Thomas[5], Jonathan[4], Israel[3], Squire[2] George[1]), was born in April 1855 in Yancey County, North Carolina. She married Tillman Boone (son of John Boone {Thomas[5], Jonathan[4], Israel[3], Squire[2] George[1]}, and Sarah Wilson), on June 15, 1863 - she was 19 and he was 22 according to the marriage record. Tillman was born in May of 1849, also in Yancey County.

There is an interesting family story about Tillman. He had an illegitimate son, James M., by Trissie's sister Martha. After the marriage, Martha brought her young son to Trissie and said: "You got the man so you can have the boy too". Trissie raised the child as her own, but James always knew who his biological mother was, and gave her name on his marriage license. Trissie and husband Tillman went on to have a total of twelve children, nine that I have a record of.

Trissie died on July 14, 1933, aged 73 years (according to her death certificate). Tillman died before her, in 1927, aged 78 years. They are both buried in Plum Branch, Boone Cemetery, in Yancey County North Carolina.

The Children of Trissie Malissa Boone and Tillman Boone			
Name	**Birth**	**Death**	**Marriage**
James M. Boone (adopted son of Martha & Tillman)	1872	1927	Minnie Hughes
Manassa Boone	1875	June 22, 1963	James Jones
James/John Nelson Boone	Oct 1879 or 1880	Feb 10 1965	Laura Dale
Cornelia Martha Boone	March 1880	August 31, 1970	Luna(r) Boone*
Hersie (Essie M.) Boone	May 16, 1882	Feb 2, 1963	Vance Carroll
Dove Boone	April 1885	October 18. 1964	Kate Hicks
Maggie Boone	July 1888		
Pansey Boone	Aug16 1891 or Sept 1890	April 17, 1975	Willie McCracken
Talmadge "Tab" Boone	Mar 11 1894	Apr 6 1973	Virgie Grindstaff
George Boone	Oct 1896		

* Luna(r) was the son of Edward and Martha McCurry Boone

Seventh Generation

Robert P. Boone

Robert P. Boone,(Jeremiah[6], Thomas[5], Jonathan[4], Israel[3], Squire[2] George[1]), was born about 1836. He married Tempie Ann Harris (born 1840, died October 7, 1917). She was the daughter of William and Anna "Emmie" (McMahan) Harris.

He served in the Civil War, enlisting on September 25, 1861 at the age of 24. He was present or accounted for until hospitalized in Richmond, Virginia on May 12, 1863 with a gunshot wound of the finger, however, place and date of wound not reported. He returned to duty on May 17, 1863, but deserted on June 17, 1863. He once again returned to duty in

JEREMIAH BOONE

November/December 1863, and was present or accounted for until captured at Hatcher's Run, Virginia on April 2, 1865. He was confined at Harts Island, New York Harbor, until released on June 17, 1865 after taking the Oath of Allegiance.

Robert Boone disappeared after serving in the Civil War. He may have moved to South Carolina.

The Children of Robert P. Boone & Tempie Ann Harris Boone			
Name	**Birth**	**Death**	**Marriage**
William McDuffy Boone	August 8, 1854	Sept 20, 1825 in Texas	1st: Nancy Caroline Washburn 2nd: Lulu Belle Shoemake
Chester M. Boone	Abt 1856		
Jerry Clayton Boone	Jan 12, 1857	Jan 27, 1947	1st: Frances Abigail Campbell 2nd: Mrs. Nettie Powell
Melvina Boone+	Dec 25, 1857	May 9, 1931	James Curtis
Laura Boone*	1860	1918 buried in Burnsville	George Silver

* A small photo of the family of George and Laura (Boone) Silver is on page 179 of *The Descendants of Israel Boone*.

Eighth Generation

Melvina Boone

Melvina Boone (Robert[7] Jeremiah[6], Thomas[5], Jonathan[4], Israel[3], Squire[2] George[1]), was born on Christmas day in 1857 in Burnsville, North Carolina. She married James Curtis on September 27, 1874, when he was 19 and she was not quite 17, according to the marriage record.

On the 1900 census, Melvina is listed as a widow with 6 children, although I only have a record of four.

Melvina died May 9, 1931, aged 73 years.

The Children of Melvina Boone Curtis & James Curtis			
Name	**Birth**	**Death**	**Marriage**
Fred Curtis	Burnsville NC		
Anna Curtis			David? Silver
Zeb Curtis			
Madge Curtis	Windom, NC	January 13, 1936	Landon Willis

Seventh Generation

Emily E. Boone

Emily E. Boone (Jeremiah[6], Thomas[5], Jonathan[4], Israel[3], Squire[2] George[1]), was born in 1832, and married Riley McMahan on August 16, 1851, when she was about 19 years old. They had at least 9 children together.

The Children of Emily E. Boone McMahan and Riley McMahan			
Name	**Birth**	**Death**	**Marriage**
Nancy C. McMahan	1853		
Mary Jane McMahan	1855		Mack Hensley
Sarah Ann McMahan	1856		Bud Sutton
Blanchey McMahan	1858		
Lucretia McMahan	1860		
Thomas C. McMahan	1863		Margaret McMahan
John Sevier McMahan	1864		Lizzie Partin
Robert P. McMahan	1866		Della Bradley
William Levi McMahan	1868		

JEREMIAH BOONE

Seventh Generation

Thomas Wesley Boone

Thomas Wesley Boone (Jeremiah[6], Thomas[5], Jonathan[4], Israel[3], Squire[2] George[1]), was born in 1840 in Burnsville, North Carollina.

He enlisted at Fort Morgan in Mobile, Alabama on January 28, 1862, and served in the 1st Battalion Confederate Infantry (also known as Forney's Regiment Confederate Infantry). He fought at Gettysburg and Chickagauga, was wounded and taken prisoner, but survived.

After the war he went to Texas, and began farming near Burton. He later had a blacksmith shop in Greenville, and built wagons and buggies. He apparently migrated to Texas with his first wife Louisia's family, the Harris'; and was later followed by some of his brothers and nephews.

About a year after Louisia's death Thomas married Mrs. Sophia (Armstrong) Sims. She was born in Rockdale, Texas, and died about 1933.

Thomas died in 1919, aged 79 years, and is buried in Medina Cemetery in Bealsey, Texas.

The Children of Thomas Wesley Boone & Louisia Harris Quzsts			
Name	**Birth**	**Death**	**Marriage**
Lawrence Boone*	October 12, 1866		
Sophie Boone	About 1869 in S.C.	Died young	
Mortimer McDaniel Boone	1871 in S.C.	October 8, 1918	Henrietta Williams
Fannie Isabel Boone	1874 in S. C.	July 25, 1936	Joseph Marion Williams

* Lawrence Boone died when his rifle went off accidently while he was hunting. He is buried in Greenville, Texas.

The Boone Connection

Seventh Generation
Baachus Boone

Baachus Boone (Jeremiah[6],Thomas[5], Jonathan[4], Israel[3], Squire[2] George[1]), was born in 1842, and apparently never married. He died in the Civil War.

Baachus enlisted as a Volunteer from Yancey County on July 3, 1861. He was 19 years old. He became a member of Company B, 29th Regiment, North Carolina Troops. He was captured on July 13 or 14, 1863 at Yazoo City, Mississippi and from there was sent to Memphis, Tennessee on July 20, 1863. He next appears on a roll of prisoners received and discharged from Groatiot Prison in St. Louis Missouri, from August 1 - 15, 1863; this roll is forwarded to Camp Morton, Indiana August 13, 1863. Finally, his name appears on a record of prisoners who died at Camp Morton On March 1, 1864. Cause of death: Typhoid fever. He is buried In Green Lawn Cemetery, #815.

Seventh Generation
Sarah Ann Boone

Sarah Ann Boone (Jeremiah[6],Thomas[5], Jonathan[4], Israel[3], Squire[2] , George[1]), was born in 1843. There is some indication that Sarah Ann never married, but a record from Family Tree Maker CD # 2 lists a Sarah A. Boone (born 1844) as marrying James P. Swofford in 1867. They are listed as having 3 children, John Henry, Elander and Zipporah. Sarah A. is listed as being buried in North Cove, North Carolina, in the North Cove Baptist Cemetery. I was unable to contact the contributor of this information for confirmation. So I do not know if this is the same Sarah Ann.

She is found on the census of 1850, and 1860. In 1870 she is 21 years old, listed as single and living with her mother. Also in this household is a child, Baccus, age 5 - probably her son. The next census (1880) she is listed as age 25, still living with her parents. In 1900 she is 58 years old, single, with 2 children - probably Baccus/Baxter (born 1855), and Ennis Clark "Dove" (born 1863).

Eighth Generation
Ennis Clark "Dove" Boone

Ennis Clark "Dove" Boone (Sarah Ann[8], Jeremiah[6],Thomas[5], Jonathan[4], Israel[3], Squire[2] George[1]), was born on March 15, 1858 according to *The Descendants of Israel Boone*, but census records seem to indicate a date closer to 1863 (see above).

He married May Lou Tom on October 13, 1880. She was born on March 20, 1862 in Washington County Texas, and died on December 30, 1932 in Colorado City Texas. They had

Jeremiah Boone

at least nine children together.

Ennis died on April 25, 1939 in Texas, presumably Colorado City.

The Children of Ennis Clark "Dove" Boone & Mary Lou Tom Boone			
Name	**Birth**	**Death**	**Marriage**
Wallie R. Boone	Jan 3, 1882	July 11, 1958	Earl Dans
Susie Evelyn Boone	March 1. 1884		J.S. Montgomery
Bigham B. Boone	Jan 12, 1886	June 1961	Medie Henderson
Lossie Raymond Boone	June 1, 1888	Jan 20, 1923	Charles Wright Hinson
Dove Ruth Boone	Feb 11, 1891		John B. Kelley
Anna Corrinne Boone	Feb 23, 1899		Jesse Jefferson "Dick" Billingley
Willie Daniel "Bud" Boone	Dec 25, 1896		Johnnie McFarland
Opal Gertrude Boone	August 22, 1902	April 30, 1921	Ted Gardner
Jack Earl Boone	May 10,		1st: Jewell Ratliff, 2nd: Dinah Taylor

Seventh Generation

McDaniel Boone

McDaniel Boone (Jeremiah[6], Thomas[5], Jonathan[4], Israel[3], Squire[2] George[1]), was born in Burnsville, North Carolina in 1845. He was another Boone blacksmith.

According to the Yancey County Marriage Index, He married Saphrona Boone on November 6, 1866, when he was 21 years old, and she was 22. Her parents were George W. Boone (son of Thomas) and Elizabeth McMahan Boone. The 1880 census indicates they lived next door to Saphrona's mother.

In *The Descendants of Israel Boone* their children are listed as: Tom, Crum, Don, Bud and Hattie.

The Children of McDaniel Boone and Saphrona Boone			
Name	**Birth**	**Death**	**Marriage**
Mary E. Boone	1867		
Eliza Boone	1869		
Jeremiah M. Boone	1871		
Hattie E. Boone*	1873		____ Beaver
Thomas W. Boone	1874		
Ella Boone	1879		John Randolph

* Hattie and her husband moved to Oregon.

Seventh Generation
Edward Boone

Edward Boone (Jeremiah[6], Thomas[5], Jonathan[4], Israel[3], Squire[2] George[1]), was born in 1845, and was another Boone blacksmith.

He married Rebecca Florence McCallister, about ten years younger than he, who was born on January 31, 1855. Her parents were Randolph McCallister and Elizabeth Hayes McCallister. Randolph was an immigrant from Ireland, and he served in the Civil War, was wounded, but survived. He was in Company B of the 63rd Tenn. Reg.

There is an interesting account on Ed Boone in *The Heritage of the Toe River Valley*, Vol. II., #234. It states that he killed a man in the 1870s (about the same time as Big Tom and Little Tom Boone were under indictment for murder). Ed escaped from jail and headed for Estelville, Virginia - but there was a price on his head. The Deputy Sheriff, Dock Hampton, (who lived on Jacks Creek) learned of Ed's whereabouts and decided to go after him. He was accompanied by the brother of the murder victim - a man named Woodfin.

They found Ed living in a large, two-story log house, and quickly handcuffed him and put him under arrest. But somehow Ed managed to create a diversion and escape to the upper floor of the house, where he had friends waiting. Ed and his friends opened fire down onto Hampton and Woodfin, eventually forcing them to retreat.

It took quite a bit of filing to remove the handcuffs, and Ed later had them repaired and a key made, so he could keep them as a souvenir, along with the pistol he used that day. These artifacts are still in the possession of descendants.

After a few years had passed, Ed Boone came in a surrendered himself to authorities.

Jeremiah Boone

He was acquitted.

Edward died in Burnsville, North Carolina, in 1904, aged 58 years.

The Children of Edward Boone & Rebecca McCallister Boone			
Name	**Birth**	**Death**	**Marriage**
Robert Lee Boone	1877	1925	Sarah Allen
William D. Boone	Aug 1883 (SC)	Abt 1899	
Hattie E. Boone	1881 or 1874	in Flat Rock, NC	Jim Cole and/or J. W. Wallen*
Lula Boone	1883		George Riddle
Margaret M. Boone	Nov 12, 1887		Charles W. Allen
Theodosia Boone	July 1892		Robert Butt
Nathan W. Boone	Feb 20, 1887	July 8, 1960	Lizzie Parrott**
Jeroan(m) Rome? Boone	Aug 18, 1890		Myrtle Hale
Lester Boone	March 1895		

*Yancey County Marriage record: "Hattie E. Boon, 19, married J.W. Wallen on August 19, 1893. In *The Descendants of Israel Boone*, her husband is listed as Jim Cole, and says she died in Flat Rock, NC.

**Lizzie (Oct 18, 1894 - Dec 5, 1963) was the daughter of Sam Parrott and Letha Boone (from death certificate).

The Boone Connection

Seventh Generation

Mary Jane Boone

Mary Jane Boone (Jeremiah^6, Thomas^5, Jonathan^4, Israel^3, Squire^2 George^1), was born in Burnsville in 1847. When she was 19 she married John C. Ramsey (age 23) on August 30, 1873. They had at least eight children. Census records indicate they lived near her father, Jeremiah Boone.

Mary Jane died about 1935, when she was 88.years old.

The Children of Mary Jane Boone Ramsey & John Ramsey			
Name	**Birth**	**Death**	**Marriage**
Laura Ramsey	Abt 1875		
William C. Ramsey		Abt 1960	
Thomas E. Ramsey			
Ed Ramsey			Emma Honeycutt
Anna Ramsey			
Hiram Ramsey			
Henry Ramsey			
Sallie Ramsey			
Kittie Ramsey			Charles Parnell

Seventh Generation
Lucretia Boone

Lucretia Boone (Jeremiah[6], Thomas[5], Jonathan[4], Israel[3], Squire[2] George[1]), was born in Burnsville, North Carolina in about 1849 or 1850. When she was 20 years old, she married Henry Butner, also age 20, on April 4, 1875. A witness on their marriage record is an S.H. Boone.

Lucretia died in 1919, according to *The Descendants of Israel Boone*.

The Children of Lucretia Boone Butner & Henry Butner			
Name	**Birth**	**Death**	**Marriage**
Laurence Boone	Abt 1877		
Mary E. Boone	Abt 1879		Tom Westall
Fred Boone		died young	
Sam Boone			
Lizzie Boone			James H. Hinsley Sr.
Sallie Boone			married & had a daughter

Headstone of J.S. Boone and wife Mary in the McIntosh Cemetery near Burnsville, North Carolina.

Seventh Generation
Jeremiah Sullins Boone

Jeremiah Sullins Boone (Jeremiah[6],Thomas[5], Jonathan[4], Israel[3], Squire[2] George[1]), was born September 20, 1854 in Burnsville, North Carolina. He was yet another Boone blacksmith, and may have been employed in another area: a J. S. Boone is on a list of Yancey County coroners for 1896-1897.

On August 24, 1873, when he was 21, he married Emily Ray who was 19 years old. They had at least 6 children.

In 1896, on November 29th, he married Mary McIntosh. He was 47, she was 30. The marriage record states he is the son of Jerry Boon and Sallie Boon, both now dead. The 1900 census, Cane River # 106, list Jerry, age 47, born Sept 1854, married to Mary, age 43, born August 1866. They have been married four years, and have had two children, neither child is living.

Jeremiah died April 24, 1932, aged 77 years, and he and Mary (died May 13, 1921) are buried in the small McIntosh Cemetery located near the Terrell House Inn in Burnsville, North Carolina. Next to them is a marker that reads: Robert (M?) Boone, July 17, 1901 - October 1902.

JEREMIAH BOONE

The Children of Jeremiah Sullins Boone & Emily Ray Boone			
Name	**Birth**	**Death**	**Marriage**
Hiram Kelse Boone	June 25, 1873	April 10, 1947	1st: Hannah Edge, 2nd: ?
Zebedee Vance Boone*	April 23, 1878	March 27, 1921	Louise Ann Williams
Fannie Louise Boone	March 4, 1881		1st: Tom Gibbs, 2nd: Sam Proctor
Daniel Dove Boone	May 25, 1882	1933	Tena Elizabeth Johnson
Samuel Sullins Boone	May 7, 1884	May 7, 1936	Irene Walters
Paul Boone	June 5, 1886	Jan 9, 1958 in Texas	Louise Boone (Zeb's widow)

* Buried in Job Cemetery, Erwin, Tennessee.

The Children of Jeremiah Sullins Boone & Mary McIntosh			
Name	**Birth**	**Death**	**Marriage**
Unknown child		died young	
Robert Boone	July 17, 1901	Oct 1902	
Nora Boone	Oct 31, 1903		Sidney Hargrove

Doctor Crumley Boone

Doctor Crumley Boone (Jeremiah[6], Thomas[5], Jonathan[4], Israel[3], Squire[2] George[1]), was born in Burnsville, North Carolina in 1859. There is an old tradition of the seventh son in a family being named Doctor, and this was done at least one other time in the Boones with Doctor Smith Pruitt Boone (Sarah Coffey[6], Jesse[4] Israel[3], Squire[2] George[1]).

He was married to Elizabeth Cole in 1893. She died less than ten years later in 1902. They had at least 3 children together.

About a year after Elizabeth's death Doctor married again, this time to Suda M. Hemphill, and they had at least 3 children.

According to census records (1880), Doctor Boone was a blacksmith.

Doctor died at age 74 on July 26, 1933.

The Children of Doctor Crumley Boone & Elizabeth Cole Boone			
Name	**Birth**	**Death**	**Marriage**
Herman D. Boone	Dec 17, 1894		Alma Guthrie
Floyd M. Boone	April 1, 1896		Nell Dean
Sophia E. Boone	Oct 1, 1898	Aug 1928	Herbert Colder
H. Franklin Boone	born in Asheville		Catherine McIntyre

The Children of Doctor Crumley Boone & Suda Hemphill Boone			
Name	**Birth**	**Death**	**Marriage**
Edna I. Boone	Sept 6, 1905	Jan 3, 1953	James M. Hyde
W. Lawrence Boone	Oct 1, 1907	Aug 25, 1915	
G. Dayle Boone	March 20, 1909		Willard J. Quinton

Chapter 24

Sixth Generation

ISRAEL BOONE

According to Alice H. Boone in "The Descendants of Israel Boone": "...there seems to be no documentary proof that this Israel Boone) was a son of Thomas". This often seems to be the case with a number of Thomas Boone's children. Also according to Alice H. Boone: "The old family Bible of this Israel's descendants contains many names and dates, but they have become almost illegible, and may have been written with the old-fashioned pokeberry ink."

Israel (Thomas^5, Jonathan^4, Israel^3, Squire^2, George^1) was born on February 1, 1804, and he married young, since his first child was born on his 18th birthday. According to census records, his wife's name is Margaret. The 1850 census lists Israel as a blacksmith.

I have a list of only three (or four) children belonging to Israel and Margaret, but because of the large number of years between their births, I wonder if there may be others.

Israel's name appears on the petition to form Yancey County in 1825, and in January 1831, his name appears on a Buncombe County Bastardy Bond. In it Polly Fergerson is charged with being the mother of a bastard child. Israel and Joseph Ray are listed as bondsmen.

In 1880, Israel and his wife are in Unicoi County Tennessee, living with their son Ervin.

The Children of Israel Boone and Margaret Boone			
Name	**Birth**	**Death**	**Marriage**
James Ervin Boone+	early 1830s		Matilda Irene Buckner
Emily Boone	Abt 1835		
Lucinda Boone	Abt 1845		
Jane Boone*			

*Jane is listed as a child in The Descendants of Israel Boone along with Ervin and Cinda. Are she and Emily the same person? The 1870 census, Cane River #56, shows a Jane Boon, age 25, as head of household. With her are listed: Gaither (1859), Kelsey (1862), John H. (1866), and Francis J. (Age 60, born 1810). Also in the same household: Minerva Harris, 26, Thursey L., 13, William, 12, and Amanda, 4.

Seventh Generation
James Ervin Boone

James Ervin Boone (Israel[6] Thomas[5], Jonathan[4], Israel[3], Squire[2] George[1]) was born on February 1, 1822 in North Carolina according to *The Descendants of Israel Boone*. However, census records seem to indicate a date in the 1830s. The 1860 census lists him as single, age 26 and living with his parents. But sometime during the next four years he married Matilda Irene Buckner, and their first child was born in 1864. They went on to have at least six more children.

Ervin is buried in the Mt. Pisgah United Methodist Church Cemetery. His son Landon and his wife are also buried in this cemetery located in Rutherford County, NC.

The Children of James Ervin Boone & Matilda Buckner Boone			
Name	**Birth**	**Death**	**Marriage**
Taylor Boone+	Abt 1864		Margaret Buckner
James Boone+	March 23, 1867	March 26, 1938	Cordelia Edith Crawford
Israel Stephen Boone+		May 13, 1896	Martha York
Etta Boone	April 8, 1870	1919	Ene(?) Boone
Landon Morris Boone+	Feb 2, 1874	Sept 24, 1953	Sarah Ann Vickers
Jeremiah Boone	Abt 1871	1916	never married

ISRAEL BOONE

The Children of James Ervin Boone & Matilda Buckner Boone			
Daniel Tucker Boone	Abt 1877	January 26, 1938	Mary English
West Boone?			
Dove Boone?			

Eighth Generation

Taylor Boone

Taylor Boone (Ervin⁷, Israel⁶ Thomas⁵, Jonathan⁴, Israel³, Squire² George¹), was born in 1864 and is probably the Taylor Boone listed in the Yancey County Marriage Records as follows: Taylor Boone, 18 - Margaret Buckner, 15, 16 Nov 1883. Together they had at least four children.

Taylor must have died before September 1899, since Yancey County marriage records list: Margaret Boone, 22, daughter of James and Sarahan Buckner, to William Brum, 18, on September 7, 1899. The 1900 census, Cane River # 178, shows Wil Broomer and wife Margaret, married less than one year in a household with the 5 Boone children listed below.

The Childlren of Taylor Boone & Margaret Buckner Boone			
Name	Birth	Death	Marriage
Sue Boone			
James Boone	March 23, 1867		
Carl Boone	June 20, 1890		
Fred Boone	Feb 1894		
Rassie Boone	Sept 1895		

109

Eighth Generation

James Boone

James Boone (Ervin[7], Israel[6] Thomas[5], Jonathan[4], Israel[3], Squire[2] George[1]), was born on March 23, 1867, and died on March 26, 1938. He married Cordelia Edith Crawford on September 18, 1890. She died soon after James, on September 18, 1890.

The Children of James Boone & Cordelia Crawford Boone			
Name	**Birth**	**Death**	**Marriage**
Emma Boone	Sept 16, 1891		
Harvey Boone	Dec 5, 1892		
Nelson Boone	Sept 25, 1894	July 5, 1896	
Quintinnia Boone	August 30, 1896		
Ethel Boone	July 18, 1898		never married
Etta Boone	May 4, 1900		
Jerry Boone	March 13, 1902		
Tennie Boone	Dec 30, 1903		
Minnie Boone	Dec 21, 1905	Sept 1952	Thomas Willis
Irene Boone	April 20, 1908	Sept 13, 1908	
Plutina Boone	July 25, 1909		Elbert Morrow
Orlie Boone	Sept 27, 1911		

Israel Stephen Boone

Israel Stephen Boone (Ervin[7], Israel[6] Thomas[5], Jonathan[4], Israel[3], Squire[2] George[1]), was the third son born the Ervin and Matilda Boone. He married Martha York in June 1890, and they had at least three children.

Israel died on May 13, 1896.

The Children of Israel Boone & Martha York Boone			
Name	**Birth**	**Death**	**Marriage**
Ernest Boone	Oct 1, 1891		Altha Cody
Dove Boone	Oct 18, 1894		Bertha Gentry
Cora Boone		died during infancy	

Eighth Generation

Landon Boone

Landon Boone (Ervin[7], Israel[6] Thomas[5], Jonathan[4], Israel[3], Squire[2] George[1]), was born around 1874, and married Sarah Ann Vickers. They had at least 10 children according to the listing in *The Descendants of Israel Boone*.

The Children of Landon Boone & Sarah Vickers Boone			
Eva Boone	May 10, 1898		Jerry Bradley
Matilda Boone	May 26, 1900		George Fincannon
Ray Boone	March 1902		Ruby Sizemore
Beatrice Boone	Dec 5, 1903		Grover Ward
John Boone			
Luke Boone			
Floyd Boone			
Lloyd Boone			
2 other children			

Chapter 25

Sixth Generation

ENOS BOONE

Enos Boone (Thomas[5], Jonathan[4], Israel[3], Squire[2] George[1]), was born in 1806 in Burke County, North Carolina. He married Jemima - last name unknown at this writing. She was born in 1820, also in Burke County.

His name appears (spelled Boon) on the petition of 1825 when the residents of Burke and Buncombe Counties sought to form a new county - Yancey. Enos Boon's name appears on the first page of the petition. In the right hand column of the same page are the names: Thos Boone and Israel Boone. Page 2, right column, has the name Eserl (Israel) Boon. Page 3 of the petition shows a T. Boon.

The 1830 census for Buncombe County shows Enos (age 20-30) and his wife (age 15-20), but no children yet. The 1850 census for Yancey shows Enos as an ironsmith. In 1860 they are on the Madison County census, and in 1870 and 1880 they are in Flag Pond Tennessee.

Enos and Jemima has at least eight children.

Children of Enos Boone and Jemima Boone			
Name	Birth	Death	Marriage
James E. Boone+	About 1833		Naoma(Oma)Candler
William R. Boone+	About 1837		Dorcas Wardrope
Elizabeth Boone	About 1841		
Mary Amanda Boone	About 1844		
Thomas Wiley Boone+	1849	Dec 10, 1890 in Madison County, NC	wed Mary Ann Willis, Feb 1870 in Flag Pond, Unicoi County, Tenn.

THE BOONE CONNECTION

Children of Enos Boone and Jemima Boone			
Marion Boone	About 1850		
Emaline Boone	About 1856		
McDaniel Boone	About 1873		Jane

Seventh Generation

James E. Boone

James E. Boone (Enos[6], Thomas[5], Jonathan[4], Israel[3], Squire[2] George[1]), was born about 1833 in Burke County, North Carolina. He can be found on the 1850 census, age 17, living with his parents.

According to the Madison County marriage register, James married Naoma Candler on September 29, 1859. The Madison County census for 1860 shows James, age 25, living with his wife. She was born in 1841, and probably died sometime before 1870, since the 1870 census shows James back living with his parents.

He served in the Civil War, and military records show he enlisted on August 12, 1861, and deserted on September 7, 1863. North Carolina pension records indicate he was wounded in 1863, so perhaps this had something to do with his desertion.

Seventh Generation

William R. Boone

William R. Boone (Enos[6], Thomas[5], Jonathan[4], Israel[3], Squire[2] George[1]), was born about 1837 in Yancey County, North Carolina. According to the Madison County marriage register, he married Dorcas Wardrope on March 24, 1861, and they had at least seven children.

The Children of William R. Boone & Dorcas Wardrope Boone			
Name	Birth	Death	Marriage

114

The Children of William R. Boone & Dorcas Wardrope Boone			
Enos Boone	1867		
Thomas Boone	1870		
Daniel Boone	1873		
James E. Boone	1875		
William R. Boone	1877		
Hulda Boone	1879		
Mollie Boone	1886		

Seventh Generation

Thomas Wiley Boone

Thomas Wiley Boone (Enos[6], Thomas[5], Jonathan[4], Israel[3], Squire[2] George[1]), was born around 1848 in Yancey County, North Carolina.

He married Mary Ann Willis (born in 1852), in February of 1870, and they had at least 6 children. They apparently lived with Thomas' parents in Flag Pond, Tennessee during the early part of their marriage, but later moved to Madison County, North Carolina.

Thomas died relatively young, on December 10, 1890, in Madison County, North Carolina. Following his death, Mary Ann and the children moved back to Flag Pond, Tennessee. She died on May 3, 1907, in Madison County, North Carolina, aged about 55 years.

The Children of Thomas Wiley Boone & Mary Ann Willis Boone			
Name	**Birth**	**Death**	**Marriage**
Sylvanus Columbus Boone*	Dec 14, 1870 in Tenn.	Sept 15, 1935 in Arkansas	Susan Alice Silver
McDaniel Boone	1873		
Margaret Boone	1875		
Thomas W. Boone	1877		
Diah C. Boone	Abt. 1879		
Lewis Oscar Boone*	Abt. 1884	1963	

*There are stories about Sylvanus and Lewis in the Madison County, North Carolina Heritage Book.

Chapter 26

Sixth Generation

SUSANNAH BOONE

Susannah Boone (Thomas[5], Jonathan[4], Israel[3], Squire[2] George[1]), was born early in the 1800's - about 1805, but possibly as early as 1800. She was probably the first daughter born to Thomas Boone and his wife Elizabeth, but could also be a daughter-in-law (see below).

She has proven to be an interesting person to research. She had at least 10 children, some or all of them illegitimate. Her first child, Nathan was born when she was between 22 and 27 years old, depending on which birth date is correct. She lived in the household of her parents (or in-laws) for many years, and her children were enumerated with their offspring on the census.

An interesting account on Nathan can be found in *The Heritage of the Toe River Valley* #583. It states that his mother is a Susannah Anderson, but Bastardy Bonds lists Susannah Boone. It is possible that Susannah Anderson married into the Boone family but I have no records to prove this. She may be a *daughter-in-law* of Thomas, enumerated with his family on the census.

She is also mentioned several times in the Yancey County court records in reference to her illegitimate children.

Children of Susannah Boone			
Name	**Birth**	**Death**	**Marriage**
Nathan Ray Boone+	Aug 20, 1827		Mary "Polly" Kuhn
Elizabeth Boone	About 1830		
John Phagan Boone+	About 1833		
Eliza Boone	About 1835		

Children of Susannah Boone			
George W. Boone+	About 1840	Feb 17, 1863	
Burton Boone+	About 1842		
William Riley Boone+	About 1844		
Luiza Boone	About 1847		
Mary E. Boone	About 1851		William Blankenship?*
Cordelia Boone	About 1852		
James Boone	About 1858		Mary Jane Deyton

* Yancey County marriage records show Mary E. Boon, 19, marrying William Blankenship, 24, on 30 June 1872. This puts Mary with a birthdate of about 1853. Is this the same Mary?

Seventh Generation

Nathan Ray Boone

Nathan Ray Boone (Susannah[6], Thomas[5], Jonathan[4], Israel[3], Squire[2] George[1]), was born on August 20, 1827. He was the son of Susannah Boone and William (Billy) Ray. His father's will of 1879 recognized Nathan as his son. Also, a Bastardy Bond of 1832 in Buncombe County lists Nathan's father as a William Rhea.

There is a story which says that when Nathan was just a few years old, Susannah sent word to William Ray to come and get this boy or I will throw him in the creek. William's wife Jane did go get Nathan and he lived with them until he was about 9 years old. He then went to live with his grandfather, Thomas Ray. Then, at about age 16, he returned to live at his father's house.

In 1847, while at a camp meeting in Rutherford County (one account says he was visiting his mother Susannah), he met the woman that was to become his wife, Mary "Polly" Kuhn. They married and lived near Pensacola, North Carolina. .

Nathan served in the Civil War in the 16th North Carolina Regiment from May 6, 1861 until discharged on December 21, 1861. This was due to an injury to his arm. (I wonder if he got home in time for Christmas!)

In the Yancey County Minutes of the County Court of Pleas and Quarter Sessions is the following:

Jan 1863   Dr. Anderson is appointed to wait on those with smallpox and make his own by-laws. A committee on the problem is to consist of N.B. (Nate "Boone") Ray...

Later the record shows that Nate Boone Ray was paid $50.00 for guarding the smallpox patients at Pensacola in 1863.

The Children of Nathan Ray Boone & Mary Kuhn Boone			
Name	**Birth**	**Death**	**Marriage**
Cordelia Boone	Abt. 1849		J.L. Dixon? *

* see Cordelia, the child of Susannah.

Seventh Generation

John Phagan Boone

John Phagan Boone (Susannah[6], Thomas[5], Jonathan[4], Israel[3], Squire[2] George[1]), was born about 1833 in Yancey County, North Carolina. A court record of 1845 orders that John Phagan, illegitimate son of Susannah Boon be bound to Charles Burleson.

On the 1850 census, John Phagan is 17 years old, and living with his half-brother Nathan.

Seventh Generation
George W. Boone

George W. Boone (Susannah[6], Thomas[5], Jonathan[4], Israel[3], Squire[2] George[1]), was born about 1840 in Yancey County, North Carolina. I have no record to indicate who his father was. George W. appears on the 1850 census, age 10, living with his mother; and on the 1860 census, age 21, still living with his mother.

He too, served in the Civil War, and the record states that he lived in Madison County prior to enlisting at age 21, on August 13, 1861. He was in Company D, 29th Regiment. He died, like so many that served, not of combat wounds, but of disease. Smallpox took his life in Cleveland, Tennessee on February 17, 1863.

I am assuming, based on the birth date, census and military records that this George W. is Susannah's son. However, I have discovered another George W. who doesn't seem to fit anywhere. He is on the Buncombe County 1880 census, age 45 (born about 1835), a blacksmith married to Martha, age 30. They have 6 children, Hannah, (1870), Adolphus (1871), Mary (1873), Hattie (1873), Robert (1876), and Hubard (1879). Perhaps he is the same as the following George:

This George W. Boone was born about 1838 in Yancey County. He resided in Madison County prior to enlisting in Co. B., 16th North Carolina Regiment, on April 29, 1861, at age 23. He is listed as present or accounted for through February 21, 1865, so he could have survived the war. Perhaps someone reading this account will know where this George Boone fits into the family tree.

Seventh Generation
Burton Boone

Burton Boone (Susannah[6], Thomas[5], Jonathan[4], Israel[3], Squire[2] George[1]), was born in 1842 in Rutherford County, North Carolina.

He was a private in NC Troops, Company B, 5th Battalion North Carolina Calvary. He enlisted in Mitchell County at age 25, on June 27, 1862. I have found no further records on Burton Boone.

Seventh Generation

William Riley Boone

William Riley Boone (Susannah[6], Thomas[5], Jonathan[4], Israel[3], Squire[2] George[1]), was born about 1844 in Yancey County, North Carolina. The 1850 and 1860 censuses show him living with his mother.

W. Riley Boone enlisted at age 17, August 13, 1861 in NC Troops, Co. D., 29th Regiment. He resided in Madison County at the time, and he was last reported in the records of Co. D. on November 30, 1863. His pension record says he was wounded at Murfreesboro, Tennessee during that year.

The 1870 census for Yancey County lists a Riley Boone, age 24, living at Cane River #178. His wife's name is Fannie, age 23. They have children Mary (born 1867), Jane (born 1867), and Silas (born 1868). Is this the same as William Riley?

Madison County marriage records list a W.R. Boon marrying Ann Norton on October 28, 1864. Is this William Riley???

The Boone Connection

Chapter 27

Sixth Generation

CLARISSA BOONE

Clarissa Boone (Thomas[5], Jonathan[4], Israel[3], Squire[2] George[1],) was born about 1810, in Burke County, North Carolina. Like her older sister(?) Susannah, she too had many children but never married. She was 17 when her first child, Manerva, was born. Clarissa lived with her father and mother when she had her first children, and they were enumerated with Thomas and Elizabeth's children on the census.

Court records state:

February 1837	*"..minor heirs of Clarissa Boon to be brought into court."*
June 1837	*"...ordered by the court that Joel Boon, infant son of Clarissa Boon be bound to Jeremiah Boon until age 21, then he is to be given blacksmith tools.*
Fall 1837	*Court issues order to bring the minor heirs of Clarissa Boone into court.*
February 1843	*Order for the Sheriff to bring all the minor children of Clarissa Boone into court.*
Fall 1843	*Amos Boon, aged 8-9 years was bound to James Boon until he was of age, in return for 2 years of schooling, one horse saddle and bridle worth $80, four suits of clothes (two of which should be "good janes"), an axe, a good hat, and a "pare of shoes".*
October 19, 1849	*Order for the sheriff to bring minor children of Cass Boon into court.*

THE BOONE CONNECTION

Children of Clarissa Boone			
Name	**Birth**	**Death**	**Marriage**
Manerva Boone	1827		
Joyce C. Boone+	About 1832		never married?
Amos Boone+	About 1834		Mexico Ray
Thomas Boone	About 1835		
Joel Boone	About 1836		
John Boone+	About 1837		Rebecca M.

Note: Robert and Joseph Boone that I have listed as children of Thomas and Elizabeth, may possibly be sons of Clarissa.

Seventh Generation

Joyce C. Boone

Joyce C. Boone (Clarissa[6], Thomas[5], Jonathan[4], Israel[3], Squire[2] George[1]), was born about 1832. She appears on the 1850 and 1860 censuses living with her mother.

I have no record of her having married, but she did have children.

The Children of Joyce C. Boone			
Name	**Birth**	**Death**	**Marriage**
Mary J. Boone	1851		
Thomas Boone*	1857		
Amandrew? Boone	1859		

*This may be the "Little Tom" Boone wanted for murder in Burnsville. (See the chapter on Samuel Boone)

124

Seventh Generation

Amos Boone

Amos Boone (Clarissa[6], Thomas[5], Jonathan[4], Israel[3], Squire[2] George[1]), was born about 1834, and he appears in court records as having been bound to James Boon when he was about 8 or 9 years old.

He married Mexico Ray on October 7, 1852, when he was about 18 years old. At some point they moved out of North Carolina since the 1870 census shows them living next door to Amos' uncle Enos Boone in Flag Pond, Tennessee. This census indicates that Mexico was age 47, and Amos was ten years younger - age 37. However, the 1870 census lists them as being only two years apart - Amos, age 56, and Mexico age 58.

They had at least one child, a son, Robert W. Boone, born in 1854. He married Harriett E. ____, and they had children Sarah Jane (born 1874), and Joseph F. (Born 1877).

Seventh Generation

John Boone

John Boone (Clarissa[6], Thomas[5], Jonathan[4], Israel[3], Squire[2] George[1]), was born about 1837, apears on the 1850 census, age 13, living with his mother.

In 1870 he appears on the Buncombe County NC census, age 34, with wife Rebecca M., age 45.

The Children of John Boone & Rebecca M. Boone			
Name	**Birth**	**Death**	**Marriage**
Clarissa Boone	Abt. 1860		
Charles C. Boone	Abt. 1864		

THE BOONE CONNECTION

Chapter 28

Sixth Generation

JOHN BOONE

John Boone (Thomas[5], Jonathan[4], Israel[3], Squire[2] George[1]), was born in 1812. He married Sarah Wilson who was born about 1823. She was the daughter of Edward Wilson and Rachel Silver. John and Sarah are buried in the Boone cemetery located on Plum Branch, one road east of Shoal Creek. The cemetery is in back of the Plum Branch Baptist Church, up the gravel road. Their grave is marked, but the marker was put up years after they died and contain no dates. This Boone cemetery and the one on Shoal Creek are on land once owned by John Boone. He owned most of the land between Shoal Creek and Micaville. As he advanced in years, he either gave (or sold at a low price) land to his children. He said he did so for the love he had for his children, and for the care they promised him in his old age.

Also in this cemetery are: T.F. Boone (1851-1937), James Boone (son of John) and his wife Malinda Boone Smith, Tillman Boone (May 1850-1927) (son of John and Sarah), and his wife Trissie Boone (1859-1932), daughter of James and Eleanor McMahan Boone. There are also other children of John and Sarah and grandchildren of Thomas buried there.

Children of John Boone and Sarah Wilson Boone			
Name	Birth	Death	Marriage
James M. Boone+	Nov 11, 1840	July 5, 1930	Lindy (Malinda Smith) Boone
Rachel M. Boone	About 1844		Noah Carroll
Edward "Ned" D. Boone+	August 1844	Jan 1, 1925	Martha McCourry
Thomas Boone+	About 1848		Sarah Ann Thomason

Children of John Boone and Sarah Wilson Boone				
Tillman Boone	May 1849	1927	Martha Boone Hughes* Trissie Malissa** Boone
Elizabeth Boone	About 1858		John Branch
Henry/Harvey Boone	About 1856		
Mary/Polly Boone***+			Thomas B. Crissaun (Chrisawn)
Nancy Boone			Grifen Crissaun

*Tillman & Martha were not married. Martha is the daughter of James (son of Jeremiah) and Eleanor McMahan Boone.
**See Chapter 23, section on Tillman & Trissie
***Mary/Polly Boone is pictured in the book *Cabins in the Laurel* as "Aunt Polly Boone".

Seventh Generation

James (Mannon or Manuel) Boone

James M. Boone (John[6], Thomas[5], Jonathan[4], Israel[3], Squire[2] George[1]), was born November 11, 1840. He was married twice - first to Rosannah Thomas (on August 24, 1866), and next to Lindy (Malinda Smith Boone) on April 14, 1884. She was born in 1855.

He served in NC Troops, Co. B, 54th Regiment as a private. He enlisted on March 21, 1862, when he was 21 years old. He was listed as present until May 4, 1863 when he was captured near Fredericksburg, Virginia. Confined at Old Capitol Prison, Washington, DC, then transferred to Fort Delaware, May 7, 1863. Paroled at Fort Delaware and transferred to City Point Virginia, where he was received on May 23, 1863 for exchange. He returned to duty prior to September 1, 1863, but was captured again at Rappahannock Station, Virginia on November 11, 1863. He was then confined at Point Lookout, Maryland, until paroled on March 10, 1864. He was received at City Point on March 15, 1864, for exchange, and returned to duty on an unspecified date. He was severely wounded in both legs at Winchester, Virginia on September 19, 1864, and was reported in the hospital at Richmond, Virginia. Despite all this - he survived the war!

The Children of James M. Boone & Rosannah Thomas Boone			
Name	**Birth**	**Death**	**Marriage**
Mary M. Boone	Abt. 1867		
Julia L. Boone*	Abt. 1869	Jan 1, 1957	never married
Nancy L. Boone	Oct. 1873		William Black
Martha J. Boone	Abt. 1876		
Dovie Boone	Abt. 1882		

* According to her death certificate, Julia died at the State Hospital in Morganton, NC, on January 1, 1957. She was 89 years old.

The Children of James M. Boone and Malinda Smith Boone			
Name	Birth	Death	Marriage
Charlie Richmond Boone	Jan 28, 1885	Jan 5, 1968 or July 12, 1984 from tombstone	Vinnie Chrisawn
John Moore Boone	April 25, 1888	August 10, 1960	Beatrice Turbyfill
Bessie A. Boone	Abt. 1892		
Sallie K. Boone	May 1894		

James M. Boone's marker in the Plum Branch Cemetery, near Burnsville, North Carolina.

Edward's marker in the Plum Branch Cemetery, Yancey County, NC.

The Boone Connection

Seventh Generation

Edward D. "Ned" Boone

Edward Boone was born about 1844 and enlisted at Burnsville, North Carolina on March 21, 1862. He was listed as a farmer with fair complexion, light hair and was 5'9" (or 5'10") tall. He was in Captain James C.S. McDowell's Company, North Carolina Volunteers, subsequently known as Company B, 54th Regiment, North Carolina Infantry.

He was captured at Fort Stedman, Virginia, on March 25, 1865.

He appears on a roll of prisoners at Point Lookout, Maryland on March 28, 1865. He was released on June 23, 1865. He signed his name to an Oath of Allegiance to the United States, subscribed and sworn to at Point Lookout, Maryland on June 23, 1865.

Four months later, according to Yancey County marriage records, he married Martha McCourry on October 13, 1865. According to her Yancey county death certificate, she was the daughter of Silas and Hannah McCurry. She died when she was about 70 years old, on June 28, 1936. She and Edward had at least 9 children together.

Edward died on January 1, 1925, and is buried at Boonford, Boone Cemetery. The death certificates lists his age as 80.

The Children of Edward Boone & Martha McCourry			
Name	**Birth**	**Death**	**Marriage**
Joseph Bowditch Boone	Jan 1866		Sina Buchanan
Para L. Boone	1869		
Eliza Boone	1871		Marcus E. Thomas
Lunar Gaston Boone	Feb 14, 1876	July 5, 1944	Cornelia Boone (d. of Tillman)
Sarah Melissa Boone	March 11, 1878	Feb 16, 1914	Sam Carroll
Willard H. Boone	Jan 9, 1881	April 7, 1930	Sarah M. Buchanan
Mack Lindsey Boone*	March 17, 1884	Oct 18, 1954	

The Children of Edward Boone & Martha McCourry			
Fred Andrew Boone	March 1886	June 10, 1964	
Curtis Boone	Feb 1888		Mary Stephens

* Mack Lindsey Boone was hit and killed by a bus.

Seventh Generation

Thomas Boone

Thomas Boone (John[6], Thomas[5], Jonathan[4], Israel[3], Squire[2] George[1]), was born about 1848. He married Sarah Ann Thomason sometime between 1866 and 1868, according to Yancey county marriage records. Her parents were Thomas J. and Drucilla Thomason.

According to one descendant, Thomas and Sarah moved to Spartanburg, South Carolina sometime after 1880.

Thomas and Sarah had at least ten children.

The Children of Thomas Boone & Sarah Ann Thomason Boone			
Name	Birth	Death	Marriage
Adolphus A. Boone	1870		
Mary C. (Minnie) Boone	Nov 25, 1872		Joe Church
Arrie Bell Boone	April 28, 1875		Ed Hunnicutt
Lou Anna Boone	Jan 29, 1877		Wm. Arsemus Calloway
Mattie A. Boone	Oct 15, 1879	Aug 23, 1975	William Biggs

THE BOONE CONNECTION

The Children of Thomas Boone & Sarah Ann Thomason Boone			
William Latimore (Lattie) Boone	March 25, 1883		Delzie Silver
Bessie A. Boone	Jan 1885		1st: Yancey Johnson, 2nd: Alfred Edwards
John Jefferson Boone	Jan 6, 1887		Lillie Hollifield
Charles Decester Boone	January 22, 1889	August 6, 1924	Ellen Shuler Steadman
Hilliard Cleophas Boone	Nov 2, 1891	May 31, 1944	Fannie Staton

Seventh Generation

Mary/Polly Boone

Mary/Polly Boone (John^6, Thomas^5, Jonathan^4, Israel^3, Squire^2 George^1), married Thomas Chrisawn, age 20, in Yancey County in 1879. Assuming that Mary was about the same age, her birthdate would have been around 1859.

She is pictured in Murial Early Sheppard's book *Cabins in the Laurel*, opposite page 48.

Chapter 29

Sixth Generation

GEORGE WASHINGTON BOONE

George Washington ("Noah") Boone (Thomas[5], Jonathan[4], Israel[3], Squire[2] George[1]), was born in 1815, and married Elizabeth McMahan.

The 1850 and 1860 census records show them living next door to Jeremiah in Burnsville, and George is listed as a blacksmith.

They had at least 11 children together before Elizabeth appears on the 1870 census without George. The 1880 census lists her as a widow, age 50, and her son Daniel lives with her.

I do not know what happened to this George W. Boone - perhaps he was killed in the Civil War - although the war records I have found on two other George W. Boones have much later birth dates than 1815.

The Children of George W. Boone and Elizabeth Boone			
Name	**Birth**	**Death**	**Marriage**
Mary A. Boone	About 1839		
Jeremiah Boone+	About 1842		
John W. Boone+	About 1842		
Sophronia Boone+	About 1847		McDaniel S. Boone (son of Jeremiah & Sarah)
Hannah E. Boone	About 1849		
Hester Jane A. Boone	About 1852		
Margaret Cordelia Boone	About 1855		J.L. Dixon?

The Children of George W. Boone and Elizabeth Boone			
Terrissa/Tempie Ann Boone	About 1856		
Sarah Boone	About 1857		W.C. Woodfin
Daniel/McDaniel Boone	About 1859		Laura Delaney
Aletha Boone+	May 29, 1864		Samuel H. Parrott

Seventh Generation
Jeremiah Boone

Jeremiah Boone (George W.[6], Thomas[5], Jonathan[4], Israel[3], Squire[2] George[1]), was born about 1842. He was a farmer before he served in NC Troops, Company E, Sixth Regiment as a private. He enlisted on May 1, 1861 in Yancey County, and was present or accounted for until he was discharged on January 21, 1862 due to "chronic rheumatism".

Seventh Generation
John W. Boone

John W. Boone (George W.[6], Thomas[5], Jonathan[4], Israel[3], Squire[2] George[1]), was born about 1844. He served in North Carolina Troops Company B, 29th Regiment as a Private. He resided in Yancey County and enlisted at age 17 on July 3, 1861. The last time he is reported in the records of that company is on April 15, 1863. No further records.

Seventh Generation
Sophronia Boone

Sophronia Boone (George W.[6], Thomas[5], Jonathan[4], Israel[3], Squire[2] George[1]), was born in 1847 and married McDaniel S. Boone, (the son of Jeremiah), on November 6, 1866. She would have been about 19 years old. Since her father and Jeremiah lived next door to each other, she and McDaniel probably grew up together as neighbors before becoming husband and wife.

John Boone

Seventh Generation

Aletha Boone

Aletha Boone (George W.[6], Thomas[5], Jonathan[4], Israel[3], Squire[2] George[1]), was born May 29, 1864. She married Samuel H. Parrott on October 5, 1878, after which they apparently went to live with his parents, James and Ann Parrott, (according to the 1880 census). At that time they are listed as having one son, Dolph, born in 1879.

Aletha died on January 12, 1947 and is buried in the Hyatt Cemetery at Windom.

The Boone Connection

Chapter 30

Sixth Generation

SAMUEL BOONE

Samuel Boone (Thomas[5], Jonathan[4], Israel[3], Squire[2] George[1]), was born in 1816, and the Caldwell County census of 1850 states that he was born in Tennessee. He was a farmer. His first wife's name was Polly (born about 1820), and they are probably buried in the Boone cemetery off Shoal Creek Road. The tombstones there are:

Samuel T. Boone
"Beloved one forever" (no dates)

Polly
"Gone but not forgotten" (no dates)

Thomas Boone, "Big Tom", (son of Samuel and Polly),
March 29, 1849 - Dec. 1, 1876
(see following section on "Big Tom")

Miranda (Nancy Miranda Nicols, wife of Big Tom),

April 22, 1848 - Jan 21, 1921

Thomas S. Boone (son of Big Tom)
1876 - 1947

L. Belle Hutchins (wife of Thomas S. Boone)

W.J. Hensley

THE BOONE CONNECTION
Died Nov 20, 1903, age 65

Cordelia Boone
Died Jan 10, 1906, age 63

Samuel and Polly lived in Tennessee for a few years, between about 1845 and 1848. By 1850 they are back on the census in Caldwell County, North Carolina, and his father Thomas is listed as living with them.

Samuel enlisted in NC Troops, 6th Regiment, Company E, on May 1, 1861 in Yancey County. Military records show he was present or accounted for until discharged on August 2, 1862 by reason of being overage.

Samuel's second wife was Sarah Randolph, according to Yancey County marriage records. They married on October 4, 1890, so first wife Polly must have died sometime between 1880 (when she appears on the census, age 53) and 1890.

An account in *The Heritage of the Toe River Valley*, Vol. II, #234, states that Sam Boone was quite a humorist, and that some of his jokes are still heard in the county.

The Children of Samuel Boone and Polly Boone			
Name	**Birth**	**Death**	**Marriage**
Susan Boone+	Sept 18, 1842	Dec 11, 1939	Jeremiah Hughes
John A. Boone+	About 1842	August 22, 1861	
Mary E. Boone	About 1844 (or 1846)		
Nancy Boone	About 1845		
Mary Ann C. Boone	About 1847		
William Boone	About 1848		
Thomas "Big Tom" Boone+	March 29, 1849	1921 in Portland Oregon	1st: Nancy Miranda Nichols 2nd: ? In Portland
Minna Boone	About 1852		
John Nelson Boone	1870		1st: Willie Ray 2nd: Lula Davis

Seventh Generation
Susan (Susannah) Boone

Susan Boone (Samuel[6] Thomas[5], Jonathan[4], Israel[3], Squire[2] George[1]), was born September 18, 1842. She married Jeremiah Hughes on August 29, 1869, when she was almost 27 years old. Their son, Thomas Greenberry Hughes (b. 1880 in Yancey), married Lena Loretta Bowman, and their family is detailed in *Unicoi County Tennessee And Its People 1875-1995*.

Susan had a long life, dying on December 11, 1939 at the age of 97! She is buried in the Hughes Cemetery at Brush Creek.

Seventh Generation

John A. Boone

John A. Boone (Samuel[6],Thomas[5], Jonathan[4], Israel[3], Squire[2] George[1]), was born about 1842. He was 19 years old, and living in Yancey County when he enlisted in Co. C, 16th North Carolina Regiment on May 1, 1861.

He died less than four months later on August 22, 1861, in a hospital in Valley Mountain, Virginia. The cause of death was not reported.

According to family accounts, he left behind an infant daughter, Mary Jane. He and the baby's mother, Mary Carroll, were never married.

The Child of John A. Boone & Mary Carroll			
Name	**Birth**	**Death**	**Marriage**
Mary Jane Boone	April 8, 1861	October 24, 1935	James C. Thomas

The Boone Connection

Seventh Generation

Thomas "Big Tom" Boone

Thomas Boone (Samuel[6], Thomas[5], Jonathan[4], Israel[3], Squire[2] George[1]), was born on March 29, 1849. He is one of the more colorful Boones!

Thomas worked as a farmer, and married Nancy Miranda Nichols on January 19, 1868, when he was about 19 years old. They lived next door to his parents.

The family story on Thomas "Big Tom" Boone is as follows:

" Big Tom" Boone did not die in 1876, as inscribed on his tombstone, nor is he even buried in the Boone cemetery (mentioned in the beginning of this chapter). The grave is empty.

Big Tom and Little Tom Boone, a cousin (possibly the son of Joyce C. Boone, see chapter on Clarissa), allegedly murdered two men and were put in jail awaiting trial. However, they managed to escape and walked to Knoxville, Tennessee. Once there, they split up, with Little Tom heading to Texas, and Big Tom to Oregon.

Apparently "Big Tom" stayed in contact with his family, since they knew he was in Oregon, and that he changed his name to George Brown. He married again and in 1900 had one child, a daughter. He died in 1921 in Portland, Oregon.

According to article # 234 in *The Heritage of the Toe River Valley, Vol II*, Little Tom Boone was convicted of killing Sam Butner around 1876 or 1877, following which he fled to Texas. He apparently lived the rest of his life there, married, raised a family, and died around the 1930s. Following his death, a lawyer came to Yancey County searching for his heirs. It seems that Tom had left a wife and child in North Carolina when he fled to Texas - who never heard from him again. But he remembered them in his will - dividing his holdings between his two families. His land went to his Texas heirs, and his money was sent to his North Carolina family.

He was said to have confessed on his death bed that Ed Boone had killed Butner - not him.

The following is from the reward poster for Big Tom and Little Tom, courtesy of Sandra Fender:

$300.00 REWARD

The Governor of North Carolina has issued two several proclamations, offering one hundred dollars reward each, for the apprehension and delivery of Thomas Boon Sr., who stands convicted of the murder of S.T. Butner, and Thomas Boon Jr., who stands convicted, of the murder of John S. Woodfin, to the Sheriff of Yancey County, NC.

And I hereby offer a reward of one hundred dollars for the apprehension and delivery to me a Burnsville in the county of Yancey, NC, of the above Boons, or fifty dollars for either of them. The said Boons made their escape from the jail of Yancy County, on the night of Oct., 22, 1879.

Sheriff of Yancey County

DESCRIPTION:
Thomas Boone Sr. is about 28 years of age, about 5 feet 9 inches high. Weights about 175 pounds, eyes light blue, large and round, complexion fair. Has a down look, left arm stiff in the elbow and slightly crooked, rather stoop shouldered.

Thomas Boon Jr., is about 23 years old, about 5 feet 9 inches high, weighs about 150 pounds, eyes blue, hair sandy, complexion fair, teeth long and lapped.

The Children of "Big Tom" Boone & Nancy Miranda Nichols Boone			
Name	**Birth**	**Death**	**Marriage**
Minnie Boone			
Julia Boone	Abt. 1871		
Thomas Samuel Boone+	Nov 13, 1876	Sept 24, 1947	L. Belle Hutchins

Eighth Generation

Thomas Samuel Boone

Thomas Samuel Boone (Big Tom[7], Samuel[6], Thomas[5], Jonathan[4], Israel[3], Squire[2] George[1]), was born in 1876, and would have been just a baby when his father fled to Oregon. He married Belle Hutchins Boone and they had at least four children.

The Children of Thomas S. Boone & Belle Hutchins Boone			
Name	Birth	Death	Marriage
Charles Karthy Boone	Nov 18, 1907	1986	
Ethel Boone	1909	1986	
Leland Boone			
Rex Boone			Margaret Boone of Charlotte ?

Headstones of Carthy Boone and Ethel Boone in the Plum Branch Cemetery, Yancey County, North Carolina.

Chapter 31

Sixth Generation

JAMES "BIG JIM" BOONE

James Boone (Thomas[5], Jonathan[4], Israel[3], Squire[2] George[1]), my great-great grandfather, has proven to be a colorful character. Born around 1824 in Yancey County, he was a blacksmith by trade and was apparently known as "Big Jim". This nickname was probably due to his reputation as an aggressive individual and not his physique, since he was only 5' 9" tall.

It is assumed that he is the "Big Jim" who killed General Alfred Keith at a hotel in Burnsville, North Carolina in the fall of 1859. The following account is from the *Asheville News,* November 3, 1859:

"HORRIBLE MURDER IN YANCEY"

"A bloody affray occurred at Burnsville, in the adjoining County of Yancy, on Friday night last, between Big Jim Boon and Gen. A.F. Keith, which resulted in the death of the latter. The circumstances our informants state were about as follows: Keith had entered a room in a hotel about midnight, and having lighted his pipe seated himself on the side of a bed, when Boon entered the room, and after a few angry words, B.caught K. by the hair and threw him on the floor and with a large knife inflicted some nine or ten stabs in the throat, breast and back; either one of which it was supposed would have proved fatal. He expired in a few minutes after and was found weltering in his blood.

Boon made his escape and is supposed to have made for Tennessee. A reward of $100 is offered by the County Court, and the Govenor will no doubt, offer $250 more for his apprehension."

Records from the Mexican War show a 2nd Lieutenant Alfred Keith in Company D of the 1st North Carolina volunteers. The captain was Tilmon Blalock. A listing of privates under Tilmon Blalock lists a Boon, probably James' brother Robert. Could James Boone have murdered Alfred Keith because of something that happened during the war?

James was in the US Army during the Mexican War. He served in Co. K, 5th Regiment, Tennessee Volunteers, Captain Paterson's unit. He enlisted on January 18, 1848 in Elizabethton, Tennessee. But this service did not last long. In March of 1848, while en route down the Mississippi, his unit's barge was hit by a tugboat. James received a shoulder injury, and was honorably discharged in Memphis, Tennessee on September 16, 1848.

Prior to this, in 1844, James Boone had married Olivia Melvina Howell (born February 12, 1826), and they set up housekeeping on her parents farm. They appear on the Carter County, Tennessee census in 1850, with children Sarah Ann, James (John Fagan?) and Elizabeth. An account written by Haska Webb (my uncle) in the 1950s states that they lived over in Lost Cove, near Roan Mountain, in Tennessee. That area today is known as Cove Creek.

In 1850, James applied for and received a pension from the government related to this shoulder injury. The doctor who examined him at the time made note of a 5-6 inch scar on his forearm, probably incurred about nine months earlier from a Bowie knife.

James must have been quite a fighter, since another family story tells of him having a fist fight with Nathan Dempsey - another blacksmith, and boxing champion. This took place somewhere near Burnsville's Town Square, and according to these family accounts, James won. This seems remarkable since Dempsey was supposed to have been much larger physically than James.

In the 1860 census for Yancey County (Ledger Community), North Carolina, Ollie appears (without James) with children Sarah A., John F., Elizabeth, Nathan and Melvina. However, the 1860 census for McDowell County lists a James Boone, grocery keeper, born in North Carolina. He is listed at #1005 with James Neal, sheriff/jail keeper. Is this the same James - in jail for the murder of Alfred Keith?   Family accounts state that James Boone and his son John Fagan (known as "Dick") both served in the 6th North Carolina unit in the Civil War. The story goes that James was permitted to escape the McDowell County jail provided he would join the Confederate army. There is a record of a James M. Boone born in Yancey, a farmer, who enlisted in the CSA 6th NC Regiment, Co. E, at Camp Jones, Virginia on 9/4/1861. In the same unit is a John P (Phagan?)Boone, who enlisted in Mitchell County on 3/8/1862 at age 18. It is said that John joined the army to be with his father, who had become ill with typhoid fever.

John, (and probably James' brothers Robert and Joseph who were in the same unit) tried to nurse him back to health. The descendants of John Fagan say he would weep when telling how he tried to help his father recover while hiding out from the Union army somewhere around Yorktown, Virginia. It was also mentioned that he would only tell this

JAMES "BIG JIM" BOONE

story when under the influence of alcohol. James died despite these efforts, shortly before General Johnston lifted the siege of Yorktown, and John Fagan buried his father himself in an unmarked grave, (presumably near Yorktown, Virginia). In 1862 Jeremiah Boone was appointed by the court as administrator of James' estate.

While James was ill, he told his son that should his mother remarry and the stepfather prove to be mean to the family, then John should kill the new husband*. This proved to be rather prophetic, since Ollie did remarry - probably Jack Hicks, and apparently he *was* mean to the family. So John Fagan shot Jack Hicks, knocking him off his horse into a creek. He said later he was not sure if it was the shot that killed him, or the fall into the creek. At any rate, John Fagan and his family were forced to flee to the state of Virginia and hide out for a while, before returning to Tennessee.

Ollie apparently never married again, but moved back to Mitchell County, where she spent some of her remaining years. Later she lived on Roan Mountain at John Phagan's home (located on Horton Creek - burned down in 1950). Here she died on March 21, 1895. She is buried in an unmarked grave in the Julian Cemetery which is located on a hill that rises from the wheat fields on John Phagan's farm.

* There is more than one version of this story, (see "The Heritage of the Toe River Valley, #187, Editor's Note). I listed the one I believe is most probable.

| The Children of James Boone and Ollie Howell Boone ||||
Name	Birth	Death	Marriage
Sarah Ann Boone+	Abt.1844		John D. Hall?
John Fagan "Dick" Boone+	March 31,1848	1917	Eliza Julian
Elizabeth (Bettie) Boone+	1851	1900	James Washington Webb
Nathan Boone	1857		no further record
Melvina Boone+	1855		John D. Tolley

THE BOONE CONNECTION

Seventh Generation

Sarah Ann Boone

Sarah Ann Boone (James[6], Thomas[5], Jonathan[4], Israel[3], Squire[2] George[1]), was born about 1844. The only information I have that might be this Sarah Ann is a census record from Marion Township of McDowell County in 1880. This Sarah Boon (born about 1848) married John D. Hall (born about 1828) and they had at least four children

The Children of Sarah Boon Hall & John D. Hall			
Name	**Birth**	**Death**	**Marriage**
Cate Hall	Abt 1865		Wm. Lentz
John G. Hall	Abt. 1870		
James A. Hall	Abt. 1872		

Seventh Generation

John Phagan "Dick" Boone

John Phagan "Dick" Boone (James[6], Thomas[5], Jonathan[4], Israel[3], Squire[2] George[1]), was born on March 31, 1848. On March 5, 1866, a few weeks before his 18th birthday, he married Eliza Julian, daughter of James Norman Julian and Delilah Hampton.

Civil War records show: John P. Boone, Private. Enlisted in Mitchell County at age 18, March 8, 1862, for the war. Present or accounted for through February 1864 at which time he was furloughed. (Some accounts say he then joined the Union army in October 1864.)

This is consistent with family stories about John Phagan joining the army to be with his ill father. It also appears he lied about his age - since he would have been not quite 14 (!) if his birth date is correct.

According to article #492 in *The Heritage of the Toe River Valley, Vol. II,* John died in 1917, and Eliza in 1930.

JAMES "BIG JIM" BOONE

The Children of John Fagan Boone & Eliza Julian			
Name	Birth	Death	Marriage
Horah Boone*	1865		
James N. Boone	1867		Loretta Frances Tipton
Mary Boone*	1867		
Orra P. Boone	1870		
Ivan Pender Boone	1870	Feb 5, 1911 (died of TB)	Naomi Tipton
Etta Mae Boone	1881		William Maynard Forbes

*In *The Heritage of the Toe River Valley, Vol. II*, #492, a Lydia Boone (1867 - 1905) is listed as a daughter of John Fagan Boone and Sarah Eliza Julian. She married John L. Shell. Is this the same person as Mary or Horah listed above?

Eighth Generation

James N. Boone

James N. Boone (John Phagan[7], James[6], Thomas[5], Jonathan[4], Israel[3], Squire[2] George[1]), was born in 1867, and married Loretta Frances Tipton (born 1880). They had at least ten children together.

The Children of James N. Boone & Loretta Frances Tipton Boone			
Name	Birth	Death	Marriage
Bertha Boone	1898		Columbus H. Hughes
David Boone			
Lida Boone			Dewey Powell

The Children of James N. Boone & Loretta Frances Tipton Boone			
Maxie Boone			Ed Street
Corbet Boone			
Ernest Boone			
Hazel Boone			Walter Street
Florence Boone			Ennie Poseley
Herman Boone			Ted Hall
John Thyler Boone	1922		1st: _____ 2nd: Isabelle Elizabeth Pritchard

Eighth Generation

Ivan Pender Boone

Ivan Pender Boone (John Phagan[7], James[6], Thomas[5], Jonathan[4], Israel[3], Squire[2] George[1]), was born in 1871. He and his wife, Phoebe Naomi Tipton had a short, sad life together. Ivan died on February 5, 1911 of consumption (TB) - he was only about 30 years old. Less than a month later, on March 24, 1911, their young son Herman died of measles - aged 2 years, 2 months, and 6 days. Then on May 17, 1911, their daughter Mary, aged 18 months, died of consumption. I have no information at this time as to what happened to Phoebe after these sad events.

Eighth Generation

Etta Mae Boone

Etta Mae Boone (John Phagan[7], James[6], Thomas[5], Jonathan[4], Israel[3], Squire[2] George[1] , was born in 1881, and married William Maynard Forbes (born 1876). They had at least eight children.

They are listed in *Carter County Tennessee, And Its People 1796-1993*, Article # 393. They moved from Mitchell County, North Carolina to Carter County, Tennessee in 1895.

The Children of Etta Mae Boone & Maynard Forbes			
Name	Birth	Death	Marriage
Ernest Forbes			Lula Geisler
Eliza Forbes			Ross Jenkins
Emma Forbes			
Paul Forbes			Minnie Harrington
L.H. "Doc" Forbes			1st: Ruby Gallimore 2nd: Peggy Lilly
Hazel Forbes			R.Y. Foster
Marteen Forbes			
Gladys Forbes			Dudley Synder

Seventh Generation

Elizabeth (Bettie) Boone

Bettie Boone (James[6], Thomas[5], Jonathan[4], Israel[3], Squire[2] George[1]), my great-grandmother, has always been a source of fascination for me. I remember visiting her grave site with my father and his brothers when I was about 7 years old. It was in an overgrown cemetery and to my child's mind the stone appeared incomprehensibly old - almost prehistoric! Today that tombstone has been replaced with a new one, but the inscription was copied exactly: *Bettie Boone, wife of James Webb.* She was always known as Bettie Boone - not Mrs. Webb. I imagine her as an independent woman, somewhat ahead of her time.

Bettie and James Washington Webb were married in Boonford, North Carolina - probably around 1868, when she was about 17 or 18 years old.

I have never found a photograph of her, although I have one of her husband James (see page 236). I have always wondered what she looked like.

Bettie was born on August 6, 1851, and died on August 10, 1900 - four days after her birthday. For a detailed accounting of this branch of the family, with many photographs, see *The Webb Family*, by Hazel Webb Hollifield.

James Washington Webb and Bettie Boone's log cabin.
(*Photo courtesy of Hazel Hollifield*)

James Washington Webb

The Children of James Washington Webb & Bettie Boone			
Name	**Birth**	**Death**	**Marriage**
Nathan Sylvester Webb	May 21, 1869	Nov 7, 1963	Molly Hopson
Washington Lee Webb	Feb 17, 1872	Jan 21, 1955	Alice Hoilman
Liza Etta Webb	Sept 27, 1874	Sept 18, 1950	Stonewall Conley
Charlie Caleb Webb	Jan 18, 1877	Aug 11, 1920	never married
Venna M. Webb	Feb 27, 1881	Jan 3, 1917	Dock Conley
Nathaniel Webb	Aug 19, 1883	March 3, 1943	Lula Canipe
Landon Webb	March 4, 1885	March 2, 1920	Martha Ann Green
Eveline Webb	Oct 29, 1887	June 14, 1972	Curtis Green
Flora Pansy Webb	Dec 29, 1890	Dec 19, 1976	Cleveland Jones
Obie Webb	July 15, 1894		Cora Lee Ratliff

Seventh Generation

Melvina Boone

Melvina Boone (James[6], Thomas[5], Jonathan[4], Israel[3], Squire[2] George[1]), was born on November 2, 1855. On June 5, 1872, she married John D. Tolley, the son of Joseph Tolley and Frances Howell. Together they had 9 children, but there was also a boy James (born March 10, 1873), who was the son of John Tolley but not Melvina.

The Children of John D. Tolley & Melvina Boone			
Name	**Birth**	**Death**	**Marriage**
William Tolley	1874	Feb 6, 1876	
Alice Whit Tolley	1876	April 21, 1897	James Martin Bowlick
Sarah Jane Tolley	Dec 13, 1878	Jane 19, 1944	Mordecai Frank Febuary
John N. Tolley ?			
Lillie M. Tolley	Oct 7, 1883	July 3, 1955	Elkanah "Cain" Julian
Dock M. Tolley			
George Tolley	Aug 4, 1890		Hattie Gribble McCurry
Clyde A. Tolley	Feb 17, 1893		lst:? 2nd: Josie Harris
Frank (Lunnie) Tolley	Feb 17, 1897		Bessie ____

THE BOONE CONNECTION

Eighth Generation

Alice Whit Tolley

Alice Whit Tolley (Melvina[7], James[6], Thomas[5], Jonathan[4], Israel[3], Squire[2] George[1]), was born in 1876, and married James Martin Bowlick (March 14, 1872 - December 25, 1953). Alice was only about 21 when she died on April 21, 1897, so she and James had only one child, a daughter, Frances.

Frances, born in 1894, also died young, about age 24, in 1918. She left a husband, Ambrose Brown and two children - Bernie, born in 1911, and Mabel, born in 1918. The birth date of Mabel suggests that Frances may have died in childbirth.

Eighth Generation

Sarah Jane Tolley

Sarah Jane Tolley (Melvina[7], James[6], Thomas[5], Jonathan[4], Israel[3], Squire[2] George[1]), was born December 13, 1878. She married Mordecai Frank Febuary (August 4, 1878 - December 7, 1943). They had eight children together.

Sarah died on January 19, 1944, about a year after her husband.

Note: I am unsure about the last name Febuary. I received the information on a computer printout, and wonder if the last name may have somehow gotten garbled into a listing of the month February. At any rate, the last name is either February or Frank.

The Children of Sarah Jane Tolley & Mordecai Frank or Febuary			
Name	Birth	Death	Marriage
William Isaac Frank/Febuary	1903	1966	never married
Charlie Penderson Frank/Febuary	1907		Mabel Elizabeth Oakes
Ruby Frank/Febuary		still-born	

The Children of Sarah Jane Tolley & Mordecai Frank or Febuary				
Cassandra Melvina Frank/Febuary	1907		John Dale Dooley
Dovie Vanella Frank/Febuary	1913		Isaac Douglas Oakes
Robert Jefferson Frank/February	Jan 21, 1915	Oct 8, 1979	Onie Lee
Florence Virginia "Fuzz" Frank/February	May 2, 1917	Feb 12, 1977	James Preston McKinney
Pansy Viola Frank/ February	April 2, 1919	Nov 6, 198	Abraham Lincoln "Link" Miller

Eighth Generation

Lillie M. Tolley

Lillie M. Tolley, (Melvina[7], James[6], Thomas[5], Jonathan[4], Israel[3], Squire[2] George[1]), was born on October 4, 1883. She married Elkanah "Cain" Julian, and together they had two daughters.

Lillie died at age 71, on July 3, 1955.

The Children of Lillie M. Tolley & Elkanah Julian			
Name	Birth	Death	Marriage
Bertha Bell Julian	1905		Walter Brownlow Ollis
Flossie Julian			

The Boone Connection

Eighth Generation

George Tolley

George Tolley, (Melvina[7], James[6], Thomas[5], Jonathan[4], Israel[3], Squire[2] George[1]), was born on August 4, 1890, and married Hattie Gribble McCurry (born 1895). They had ten children.

The Children of George Tolley & Hattie McCurry			
Name	**Birth**	**Death**	**Marriage**
Edith Tolley	Aug 26, 1911		1st: ___ Buchanan, 2nd: ___ Greene
Ethel Tolley	April 13, 1913		
Georgia Tolley	July 23, 1915		
George Tolley	Dec 21, 1917		
Maxine Tolley	Feb 5, 1920		J.D. Braswell
Clara Lee Tolley	Sept 7, 1922		
Willa Jean Tolley	March 11, 1925		
Joseph Burl Tolley & Murl Tolley (twins)	March 25, 1927		
Howard Tolley	March 26, 1934		Anna J____

Chapter 32

Sixth Generation

NAOMI BOONE

Naomi Boone (Thomas[5], Jonathan[4], Israel[3], Squire[2] George[1]), was born about 1823 - 1825, and could be the child of one of Thomas and Elizabeth's sons, but I have chosen to list her as one of theirs. Like her (presumed) sisters Susannah and Clarissa, had several children but never married.

Naomi is found on the Yancey County census of 1850, age 27, and living next door to her brother, George W. Boone.

The Children of Naomi Boone			
Name	**Birth**	**Death**	**Marriage**
James D. Boone	About 1842		
Sophronia Boone	About 1845		
Sarah A. Boone	About 1847		

The Boone Connection

Chapter 33

Sixth Generation

ROBERT BOONE

Robert Boone (Thomas[5], Jonathan[4], Israel[3], Squire[2] George[1]), was born on June 27, 1823 in Yancey County North Carolina. He married Naomi Howell in 1845, about two years before he served in the Mexican War. They lived near his brother Joseph, right at the edge of the South Toe River - this is how Boonford came by its name.

Once again, the parentage of this Robert is in question. There is a J. Robert Boon found in several Civil War documents, listed as being 5 feet 11½ inches tall (according to his Oath of Allegiance). Is this the same Robert - or another? The roster of the 6th NC Troops. Co E., lists the following:

Boone, J. Robert, Private. Resided in Mitchell County and enlisted in Alamance County at age 36, June 17, 1861 for the war. Captured near Petersburg, Va., March 25, 1865 and confined at Point Lookout, Md., until released after taking Oath of Allegiance June 22, 1865.

This indicates a birth date for Robert of about 1826.

According to an 1836 Yancey County deed record (Book #1, page 155), there was a NC state grant to James Howell for 50 acres joining Henry Grindstaff's and Robert Boon's and his own. This makes Robert (born in 1823) rather young to be a land owner, but makes more sense for a Robert born around 1814. Thomas Boone is listed as having a son Robert born about 1814 in *The Descendants of Israel Boone*.

The following notes are quoted directly from the research of Sandra Fender:

"From Mexican War Pension Record:
Naomi Boon, Boonford, Yancey Co., NC, Widow of Robert Boon Private - Captain Timothy

Blalock - D - 1 NC Vols, enlisted 1848. Filed Apr. 6, 1907 at Knoxville, Tenn.

Paper dated Dec. 27, 1901, Mr. Robert Boon, Wing, Mitchell Co, NC. Are you a married man, if so to whom? Nayoma Howell.
When and where married? Married in Yancey Co. About 1845 by Isaac Wilson.
What record? The record was deposited in Yancy Co. At Burnsville NC but I think the paper was destroyed during the Civil War.
Married before? Neither of us were married before.
Children? Have 3 sons living and 7 children dead.
Samuel Boone was born 1847
Joseph Boone was born 1853
Jackson Boone was born 1867
Signed by Robert Boon on Jan 3, 1902, with his mark.

Paper dated Sept. 20, 1893:
Request for records for Robert Boon who enlisted Feb 14, 1847 in the 1st NC Vols. Company of D. Col Robt Payne and was discharged Aug 7, 1848.

Paper dated Sept 22, 1893:
Record and Pension Office
The rolls show that Robert Boon, Co D, 1st Regt. NC Vols Mex War was enrolled Jan 25, 1847 at Burnsville, mustered in Feb 15, 1847 at Wilmington NC and MO with Co. Aug 7, 1848 at Smithville NC.
Apr 30, 1847, Camargo, Mexico
June 30, 1847, Beuna Vista, Mexico
Dec 31, 1847, Arishas Mills M. Saltillo, Mexico
Feb 29, 1848, Satillo, Mexico
April 30, 1848, pap Gallos, Mexico, en route for Seralvo.

Paper dated Sept 5, 1893, Medical staement by Dr. John Stichcomb, Ledger, Mitchell County, NC.

"I have known Robert Boon personally since Nov 1887 and since, & since I met him regard him as a man physically incapacitated for obtaining a livelihood by manual labor, on account of age and infirmity. As to his property I do not think it would sell for the sum of $100.00 most likely it would not cover the mortgage of $50.00".
Statement by James C. Phillips and Wm. Willis of Ledger:
"We are near neighbors of the claimant Robt Boon and the facts set forth in Dr. J. Stichcombs certificate are true. We have for several years heard him complaining of

Robert Boone

Rheumatism and shortness of breath".
Paper dated March 22, 1870 Oath of Allegiance:
Robert Boon aged 48, resident of Mitchell. Signed with a mark.

Paper dated 26 April 1907:
Garrett Boon, age 56, of Wing, NC state:
"I am a nephew of Robert Boon and was acquainted with and Naomi Boon his widow as far back as I can remember. Naomi Boon according to my recollections or knowledge is at least 70 years old and entirely incapacitated"
James Phillips, 59, of Wing NC:
" I have known both Robert and his widow Naomi as long as I can recollect, about 45 years. Naomi boon is at least 80 years old. She was a Howell. They were married before he went to the Mexican War by a magistrate Wilson. Robert died March 15, 1907, about 95 years old".

19 April 1907:
Naomi Boon age 80 years, widow of Robert Boon. He served as a Private in the company commaned by Capt Tillman Blalock. He was 6 feet tall with blue eyes, sandy hair, fair complexion, by occupation a Blacksmith. He was born at booneford at that time in Burke County, NC. Naomi state that she was married to Robert about June 1847 by Isaac Wilson. She was Naomi Howell. She is about 80 years old and was born in 1827 in Boonford then in the county of Burke now in Mitchell. Naomi signs with her mark.

Paper dated 9 Feb 1887:
Robert Boon staes that he is 63 years old and a resident of Bakersville, Mitchell County.

Paper dated 15 April 1886:
Robert Boon states he is age 62. Places of residence since his discharge: in Mitchell and Yancey Counties near Burnsville in Yancey County for a few years and the balance of the time near Bakersville, Nc. About 6 feet tall, eyes blue, hair light and light complexion.

Paper dated March 2, 1887:
I was born at Cane River, Yancey County NC on the 27 day of June 1823. I am 64 years old in June. I am disabled by reason of lung disease the disablity was incurred at Buna Vista in 1947. My wife was Oma Howell and I was married at Snow Creek in NC in 1845. My wife is living."

Robert and Naomi and 5 of their children are said to be buried in the Snow Creek area of Mitchell County NC, with only rocks as headstones.

The Children of Robert Boone & Naomi Howell Boone			
Name	Birth	Death	Marriage
Samuel (James Samuel?) Boone	July 28, 1848	Jan 22, 1930	1st: Lula Davis 2nd: Elizabeth Tolley
Mary/Polly A. Boone	About 1852		
Jane Amanda Boone	About 1854		Jesse Wilson
James Boone	About 1856		
Joseph "Jute" Boone	About 1858	Feb 7, 1925	1st: ____? 2nd: Sarah Sparks
Delilah Boone	About 1863		
Stonewall Boone	About 1868		
Mary Belle Boone	About 1871		
Elizabeth Boone	About 1872		William Ray

Seventh Generation

Samuel (James Samuel?) Boone

Samuel Boone (Robert[6], Thomas[5], Jonathan[4], Israel[3], Squire[2] George[1]), is yet another Boone whose parentage is not really known. He was born on July 28, 1848 in Boonford, North Carolina. Family stories indicate that Samuel's birth father may have been Phagan McDaniel Young, son of George Young, who was the owner of a water-powered mill. Apparently he fathered Samuel with Naomi Howell when she was only 14, and then refused to marry her. But shortly after Samuel was born, Robert Boone married Naomi and gave Samuel his name.

Samuel married two times. First to Elizabeth Tolley, with whom he had five children, and next to Lula Davis, with whom he had seven children. Census records show Samuel with wife Elizabeth in 1870, and in 1880 he seems to have been counted twice - once living with Elizabeth and once living in the home of James Anglen at Crabtree #104, with no wife listed. The 1900 census shows him with Lula and they have been married 15 years and have had 7 children, 6 living. So Elizabeth either died between 1880 and 1883, or they divorced or stopped living together as husband and wife.

ROBERT BOONE

Samuel died on January 22, 1930. He and Lula and several of their children are buried in the Rebel's Creek Cemetery, Mitchell County, North Carolina.

The Children of Samuel Boone & Elizabeth Tolley			
Name	**Birth**	**Death**	**Marriage**
Nelson Boone+	1869	About 1936	
Charles Boone	1872		
William H. Boone	1875	1952	Florence Murdock
James M. Boone+	July 20, 1877	Dec 27, 1957	Elizabeth (Bessie) Willis
Samuel Boone	1879		

Eighth Generation

Nelson Boone

Nelson Boone (Samuel^7, Robert^6, Thomas^5, Jonathan^4, Israel^3, Squire^2 George^1) was born in 1869 in Mitchell County, North Carolina. He married twice - to Willie Ray, with whom he had four children; and to ____Lunsford, with whom he had two children.

Nelson was about 67 years old when he died in Buncombe County, North Carolina in 1936.

Children of Nelson Boone & Willie Ray Boone			
Name	**Birth**	**Death**	**Marriage**
Olga Boone	About 1905		David Miller
Beryl Boone	About 1905		___Hayes
Ray Riley Boone	July 15, 1907	Dec 7, 1988	Virginia Cynthia Cordell
Glenn Boone	May 18, 1910	April 25, 1979	Emma Holmes

The Children of Nelson Boone & ___Lunsford Boone			
Name	Birth	Death	Marriage
Ida Boone			
Harry Boone			

Eighth Generation

James Boone

James Boone (Samuel[7], Robert[6], Thomas[5], Jonathan[4], Israel[3], Squire[2] George[1]), was born on July 20, 1877, and married Elizabeth (Bessie) Willis. However, according to account # 509 in *The Heritage of the Toe River Valley, Vol II*, James was the subject of a local scandal.

When James was 26 or 27 years old he was living with his father Samuel and his stepmother Lula. In the fall of that year (1903), he began courting Annie Mae ("Tine") Howell, the 13-year-old illegitimate daughter of Dovie Howell and Robert Silver. James and Tine married soon after, at the old Boonford depot.

Tine's mother Dovie was the housekeeper for old Dr. Stinchcomb (who was unable to live independently). Eventually the two of them married - he was 69 and she was 34. Living with them at this time was Dr. Stinchcomb's adult son Paul. Paul was mentally ill and had been in and out of various hospitals. Tine lived in this household until her marriage to James Boone. Sometime prior to her marriage to James, her mother's marriage seemed to falter - with Dr. Stinchcomb and Paul moving 30 miles away to a logging camp in Nelson.

James and Tine's marriage also faltered. Only two months after the wedding, Tine left him and went to Baltimore with Paul Stinchcomb. Local gossip said that Dr. Stinchcomb and Paul had moved to the logging camp to put an end to an affair Paul was having with Tine.

James did not officially file for divorce from Tine until almost ten years later - on May 5, 1913. In the divorce papers he stated that Tine had committed adultery with Paul Stinchcomb and others. In July of that year (1913) he married Elizabeth (Bessie) Willis.

James died on December 27, 1957, and he and Bessie are buried in the Rebel's Creek Cemetery.

ROBERT BOONE

Some of Paul Stinchcomb's life is written about in *Cabins in the Laurel*. Another interesting note: Paul is said to have died when the Titanic sank in 1912 - but he has not been found on the passenger list. Would he have traveled under an assumed name?

The Children of Samuel Boone & Lula Davis Boone			
Name	Birth	Death	Marriage
Joseph Boone	March 1883		
Edward Boone	Oct 1885		
John Nathan Boone	December 5, 1889	March 12, 1960	Nola Ada ___
Milton Boone	Sept 1891	1958	Minnie M__
Willard Boone	Feb 22, 1892	Sept 24, 1927	Zina _____ .
Harry E. Boone	Dec 18, 1895		
Mamsie Boone	Jan 1897		

Seventh Generation

Joseph "Jute" Boone

Joseph "Jute" Boone (Robert[6], Thomas[5], Jonathan[4], Israel[3], Squire[2] George[1]), was born about 1858. He was a Baptist minister, apparently married twice, his second wife was Sarah Sparks.

According to his Mitchell County death certificate, Joseph died on February 7, 1925, aged 72.

There is a photograph of him in *The Heritage of the Toe River Valley*, Volume 1, page 287.

Chapter 34

Sixth Generation

JOSEPH BOONE

Joseph Boone (Thomas[5], Jonathan[4], Israel[3], Squire[2] George[1]), is the brother of Robert Boone, but their parents are still in question. However, I am listing them both as sons of Thomas, but they may instead be grandsons - possibly sons of Clarissa.

Joseph married Delilah Howell, and they can be found on the 1860 census, Ledger community, #1062 - Joseph is 25, Delila is 27. Also in the household is Martha Howell, age 65.

Joseph served in the 6th Regiment NC Troops, Company E, enlisting in Alamance County on June 27, 1861 - ten days after his brother Robert enlisted. He was 28 years old at the time. On July 21, 1861 he was wounded at the battle of First Manassas. He was present or accounted for until he deserted on March 27, 1862. Company muster roll dated Jan-Feb 1864 states that he was "present in arrest".

Joseph survived the war, and the 1870 census shows him, age 36, living at Crabtree #73, with his wife, also age 36. The 1880 census shows him at Crabtree #88, age 55, with wife age 47.

A Yancey County marriage record lists: Joseph Tolley 57, Delilah Boone, 43, 11 July 1881. So it appears that Joseph may have died sometime after 1880, and Delilah remarried.

The Children of Joseph Boone & Delilah Howell Boone			
Name	**Birth**	**Death**	**Marriage**
Melvina Boone	About 1853		Samuel Fleming Young
Garrett D. Boone*	Dec 2, 1854	Aug 7, 1943	Emma Fortner
Louisa Boone	About 1868		
Martha V. Boone	May 1870		
Dora M. Boone?**	About 1872?	1929	John W. Gurley
Charles Boone	About 1878		
Mimer? Malinda? Boone	About 1878		
Lillie (Delilah)* Boone	About 1878		Wyatt Robinson*

*It may be this Garrett Boone that is shown in a photo taken about 1904 in *Images of Yancey*, page 104.

** In *The Heritage of the Toe River Valley*, Volume 1, #596, page 397, (the section on Wyatt Robinson), states that Lily Boone, daughter of Joe Boone, was Wyatt's second wife. It goes on to say that they had four children together: Calvin, Mira, Florence, and Nettie, but his wife had a daughter Dora prior to her marriage that Wyatt brought up as his own. I wonder if the Dora M. listed above may be the daughter of Lillie, and not Delilah and Joseph.

CONCLUSION

I would like to invite readers to submit any information they may have on the Boone lineage. Perhaps we can finally solve some of the mysteries of the mountain Boones.

Send information to:

Debra Webb Rogers
1840 Thacker Avenue
Jacksonville, Florida 32207

BIBLIOGRAPHY

Bailey, Lloyd Sr., *Images of Yancey, Pictorial History of a Western North Carolina County*, c.1993, Yancey History Association, Burnsville, North Carolina, Walsworth Publishing Company.

Bailey, Lloyd Sr., *The Heritage of the Toe River Valley*, Vol. I, c. 1994, Walsworth Publishing Co., Inc.

Bailey, Lloyd Sr., *The Heritage of the Toe River Valley*, Vol. II, c.1998, Walsworth Publishing Co.,Inc.

Boone, Alice H., *The Descendants of Israel Boone*, c. 1969, McCann Publishing Co.

Boone, Alice H., *More Descendants of Israel Boone*, c. 1984, McCann Publishing Co.

Brawley, James S., *Rowan County, A Brief History*, c. 1977, North Carolina Division of Archives and History.

Faragher, John Mack, *Daniel Boone, The Life and Legend of an American Pioneer*, c. 1992, Henry Holt and Company, Inc.

Hollifield, Hazel Webb, *The Webb Family*, c.1989, Celo Valley Books, Burnsville, North Carolina.

Hodges, Dr. J.E., *Jesse Boone, Son of Israel Boone*, copy of this pamphlet in Davie County Public Library, Mocksville, North Carolina.

Iobst, Richard W., *The Bloody Sixth, The Sixth North Carolina Regiment Confederate States of America,* c.1965, North Carolina Centennial Commission, reprinted by Old Soldier Books, Inc., Gaithersburg, Maryland.

Kephart, Horace, *Our Southern Highlanders*, c. 1913, reprinted 1992, MacMillan Publishing Co.

Index

1st Battalion Confederate Infantry, 97
1st Nc Vols. Company of D, 162
1st Regt. NC Vols Mex War, 162
Alexander
    Nancy, 57
Allen
    Charles W., 101
    Hannah, 50
    Jonathan, 20
    Mary, 57
    Sarah, 101
Anderson
    Dicy E., 56
    Dr., 119
    Susannah, 117
Anglen
    James, 164
Arishas Mills M. Saltillo, Mexico, 162
Aunt Chainey, 57
Austin
    Samuel, 81
Bailey
    John "Yellow-Jacket", 76
Bakersville, NC, 163
Ball
    Arthur, 89
    Benjamin, 91
    Essie, 89, 91
    Jane, 91
    William, 91
    William Garfield, 89
Beaver
    unknown, 100
Beuna Vista, Mexico, 162
Biggs
    William, 133
Billingley
    Jesse Jefferson "Dick", 99
Black
    William, 129

Blalock
- Captain Timothy, 162
- Capt Tillman, 163
- Tilmon, 146

Blankenship
- William, 118

Bogle
- Susan, 58, 59

Boon
- Amos, 72, 123-125
- Big Jim, 85, 145
- Cass, 123
- Gaither, 108
- Garrett, 163
- J. Robert, 161
- James, 123,125
- Jeremiah, 123
- Jerey, 82
- Jerry, 84, 104
- Joel, 123
- John H., 108
- Kelsey, 108
- Mary E., 118
- Naomi, 159, 161-163
- Robert, 146, 161-163
- Sallie, 104
- T., 76
- Thomas, Jr., 142,143
- Thomas, Sr., 142
- Thomas,Jr., 143
- Thos., 76

Boone
- Eleanor McMahan, 127
- J. S. , 104
- Margaret Clement, 79
- Mary Jane, 84, 102, 141
- Adolphus, 120
- Adolphus A., 133
- Albert, 24
- Aletha, 136

Alfred Joel, 69
Alice, 13, 14, 16, 39, 44
Alice H., 107
Allen, 27, 28
Altha, 86, 88
Altha Jane, 88, 91
Altha Jane McMahan, 88
Amandrew, 124
Amos, 72, 124, 125
Andrew, 80
Andrew Jackson, 88
Anna, 21, 31
Anna Corrinne, 99
Arrie Bell, 133
Aunt Polly, 128
Baachus, 83, 98
Baccus, 98
Barbara Ellen, 88, 90
Beatrice, 112
Belle Hutchins, 139, 143
Benjamin, 3
Bertha, 149
Beryl, 165
Bessie A., 134
Bettie, 147, 151, 152, 154
Big Tom, 100, 140-143
Bigham B., 99
Bud, 99
Burton, 118, 120
Bussie Varina, 69
Carl, 109
Caroline, 81, 83
Carrie Idella, 88, 91
Celia, 21, 37
Charles, 165, 170
Charles Decester, 134
Charles Karthy, 144
Charlie Richmond, 130
Chester M, 95
Cinda, 107

Clarissa, 76, 77, 123-125, 159, 142, 169
Cora, 111
Corbet, 150
Cordelia, 118, 119, 140
Cornelia, 132
Cornelia Martha, 94
Cornelius, 84
Crum, 84, 98,99,106, Addenda VII
Curtis, 133
Daniel, 5, 9, 13,14, 19-21, 23-26, 31, 39, 43, 75, 115, 135
Daniel Asbury, 51
Daniel Dove, 105
Daniel Tucker, 109
Daniel/McDaniel, 97-99, 100, 114, 116, 136, Addenda III, VI, VII
David, 149
Delilah, 164, 169, 170
Deszel, 27
Diah C., 116
Dick, 146, 148
Doctor Crumley, 84, 106
Doctor Smith Pruitt, 106
Don, 99
Dora, 170
Dora M., 170
Dorcas Wardrope, 113-115
Douglas Lorenzo, 88
Dove, 94, 98, 99,105, 109, 111
Dove Ruth, 99
Dovie, 129
Ed, 132, 142
Edna I. , 106
Edward, 9, 93, 99, 132, 133, 168
Edward A., 84
Edward "Ned" D., 127, 132
Eleanor, 45, 57, 58, 71
Eleanor McMahan, 127, 128
Elendor/Nellie McMahan, 85, 86
Elijah, 67, 68, 70
Elijah M., 27, 70
Eliza, 100, 117, 132

Eliza Julian, 147, 148, 149
Elizabeth, 9, 14, 16, 23-27, 27, 39, 71, 75, 77, 79-81, 84, 113, 117, 123, 128, 146, 159
Elizabeth (Bessie) Willis, 165
Elizabeth (Bettie), 147, 151, 152, 154
Elizabeth /Bettie, 164
Elizabeth Boone, 14
Elizabeth Cole, 105
Elizabeth Kincaid Warlick, 67, 70
Elizabeth McMahan, 99, 135, Addenda
Elizabeth Tolley, 164,165
Elizabeth "Betsy", 28
Ella, 100
Emaline, 114
Emily, 72, 107
Emily E., 83, 95
Emma, 110
Ene, 108
Ennis Clark "Dove", 84, 97
Ennis Clark "Dove", 98, 99
Ennis "Dove", 84
Enos, 113-115, 125
Enos "Knock", 77
Ernest, 111, 150
Eserl, 113
Ethel, 110, 144
Etta, 108, 110
Etta Mae, 149, 150, 151
Eva, 112
Fannie Isabel, 97
Fannie Louise, 105
Florence, 150
Floyd, 112
Floyd M., 106
Fred, 103, 109
Fred Andrew, 133
G. Dayle, 106
Garrett, 163, 170
Garrett D., 170
George, 1, 5, 9, 13, 94, 120

George IV, 3
George Riley, 53
George W, 84, 99, 159, Addenda
George W., 84, 118, 120
George Washington, 135
George "Noah" Washington, 77
Glenn, 165
H. Franklin, 106
Hannah, 9, 21, 120
Hannah E. , 135
Harriett Eleanor, 70
Harriett Elizabeth Jopling, 69, 70
Harry, 166
Harry E., 168
Harvey, 110
Hattie, 99, 120
Hattie E., 99, 100, 101
Hazel, 150
Henry/Harvey, 128
Herman, 150
Herman D., 106
Hersie (Essie M.), 94
Hester Jane A., 135
Hilliard Cleophas, 134
Hiram Kelse, 105
Horah, 149
Hubard, 120
Hulda, 115
Ida, 166
Ida Cornelia, 70
Ida Virginia, 69
Irene, 110
Isabella, 56, 65, 67
Israel, 5, 9, 13, 14, 16, 21, 24, 25, 27, 39, 44, 77, 107, 113
Israel Stephen, 108, 111
Israel "Jack", 28
Israel's, 13
Ivan, 150
Ivan Pender, 149, 150
J.G., 80

Jack Earl, 99
Jackson, 162
Jacob, 28
James, 3, 43, 77, 83, 86, 108-110, 118, 127, 146, 164-166
James "Big Jim", 145
James (Big Jim), 85
James A., 88
James D., 159
James E., 81, 83-86, 113, 114
James Ervin, 107, 108, 109
James M, 92
James M., 87, 93, 127, 129, 130, 146, 165
James Mannon, 129, 130
James N., 149
James/John Nelson, 94
Jane, 107
Jane Amanda, 164
Jemima, 45, 63, 77, 113
Jeptha (Jesse), 45, 51
Jeremiah, 76, 77, 81, 84, 85, 89, 90, 101, 109, 128, 135, 136, 147, Addenda
Jeremiah M., 100
Jeremiah Sullins, 75, 84, 104, 105, Addenda
Jeroan(m), 101
Jerry, 110, 104
Jerry Clayton, 95
Jesse, 6, 13, 14, 16, 19, 23, 24, 26, 27, 29, 39, 43, 71
Jeter Nathan, 89
Joe, 170
Joel, 45, 123, 124
Joel M., 71, 72
Joel Nixon, 58, 67
John, 3, 23, 24, 28, 45, 52, 56, 58, 65, 67, 70, 83, 92, 112, 124, 125, 127
John A., 140
John A. , 141
John Benjamin, 69
John F, 146
John Fagan, 146, 149
John Fagan "Dick", 147
John Jefferson, 134
John Moore, 130

John Nathan, 168
John Nelson, 94, 140
John P. , 72, 148
John Phagan, 117, 119, 147
John Phagan "Dick", 148
John Thyler, 150
John W. , 135, 136
John "Johnny", 77
Jonathan, 9, 13, 14, 16, 19-21, 23, 39, 43, 44, 51, 71
Jonathan Jr., 24
Joseph, 3, 77, 124, 161, 162, 167, 169, 170
Joseph Bowditch, 132
Joseph F. , 125
Joseph "Jute", 164, 168
Joyce C., 124, 142
Joyce C. , 124
Julia, 143
Julia L., 129
L. Belle Hutchins, 139, 143, 144
Landon, 111, 112
Landon Morris, 108
Laura, 95
Laurence, 103
Lawrence, 97
Leland, 144
Lester, 101
Letha, 101
Lewis Oscar, 116
Lida, 149
Lillie, 170
Lillie (Delilah), 170
Lily, 170
Lindy (Malinda Smith , 129
Lindy (Malinda) Smith, 127
Little Tom, 100, 124, 142
Lizzie, 103
Lloyd, 112
Loretta Frances Tipton, 149
Lossie Raymond, 99
Lou Anna, 133

Louisa, 170
Louisa Cerealda, 53
Louise, 105
Louisia Harris, 97
Lucinda, 107
Lucretia, 84, 103
Luiza, 118
Luke, 112
Lula, 101, 166
Lula Davis, 140, 164, 168
Luna(r), 94
Lunar Gaston, 132
Lydia, 149
Mack Lindsey, 132
Maggie, 94
Malinda, 127, 170
Mamsie, 168
Manassa, 94
Manerva, 123, 124
Margaret, 55, 67, 81, 83, 85, 107, 109, 116, 144
Margaret Cordelia, 135
Margaret M., 101
Marion, 114
Martha, 13, 92, 120, 128
Martha (Patsy) Sinclair, 71
Martha A, 86
Martha A., 72, 87
Martha J., 129
Martha McCurry, 93, 132, 133
Martha V. , 170
Mary, 1, 3, 9, 24, 43, 45, 72, 83, 88, 120, 149, 150
Mary A., 135
Mary A. (Polly), 25
Mary Amanda, 113
Mary Ann C., 140
Mary Ann Willis, 113, 115, 116
Mary Belle, 164
Mary C. , 133
Mary E., 86, 100, 103, 118
Mary E. , 102, 140, Addenda VII

Mary Early?, 80
Mary Isabelle, 69
Mary J., 66, 84, 124
Mary Jane, 84, 102, 118, 141
Mary M. , 129
Mary Martha Malissa, 88, 89
Mary "Polly" Kuhn, 117, 118
Mary/Polly, 128, 134
Mary/Polly A., 164
Matilda, 112
Matilda Irene Buckner, 107, 108
Matilda?, 80
Mattie A., 133
Maxie, 150
May Lou Tom, 98, 99
McDaniel, 99, 100,114, 116, Addenda VII
McDaniel S., 84, 135, 136
Melinda, 72
Melvina, 95, 146, 147, 155, 170
Melvina , 94
Mexico Ray, 124
Milton, 168
Mimer? Malinda?, 170
Minna, 140
Minnie, 70, 110, 143
Minnie M, 168
Mollie, 115
Mortimer McDaniel, 97
Nancy, 21, 25-27, 52, 67, 128, 140
Nancy L., 129
Nancy Miranda Nicols, 139
Naoma Candler, 114
Naomi, 77, 159, 163
Nathan, 19, 117, 119, 146, 147
Nathan Ray, 117-119
Nathan W. , 101
Nellie, 70, 84
Nelly, 86
Nelson, 110, 165
Nola Ada, 168

Nora, 105
Olga, 165
Ollie Howell, 77, 147
Opal Gertrude, 99
Orlie, 110
Orra P., 149
Pansey, 94
Para L. , 132
Paul, 105
Plutina, 110
Polly, 25, 77, 128, 140
Quintinnia, 110
Rachel, 21, 27, 39, 40, 45, 49, 50
Rachel Elizabeth, 80
Rachel M., 127
Rassie, 109
Ray, 112
Ray Riley, 165
Rebecca, 14, 43
Rebecca M., 125
Rex, 144
Robert, 77, 81, 88, 95, 105, 120, 124, 125, 161, 163, 164, 169
Robert (M?), 104
Robert Nelson, 67, 69, 86, 88, 91
Robert P., 83
Robert P. , 94, 95
Robert W., 125
S.H., 103
Sallie, 14, 16, 103
Sallie K., 130
Sam, 103, 140
Samuel, 3, 9, 53, 75-77, 124, 139, 140, 162, 164, 165, 168
Samuel (James Samuel?), 164
Samuel Sullins, 105
Samuel T. , 139
Saphrona, 99
Saphronia, 84
Sarah, 3, 5-7, 9, 14, 21, 28, 29, 136
Sarah (Sallie), 16
Sarah A., 55, 84, 98, 159

Sarah Ann, 23, 24, 83, 84, 88, 90, 98, 146-148
Sarah Ann Thomason, 127, 133
Sarah Jane, 24, 125
Sarah L., 56, 67
Sarah McMahan, 16, 19, 21, 23, 27
Sarah Melissa, 132
Sarah Morgan, 3, 5, 6, 9, 12, 13, 14, 43
Sarah Sparks, 164, 168
Sarah Wilson, 77, 93, 127
Sophia (Armstrong) Sims, 83, 97
Sophia E., 106
Sophie, 97
Sophronia, 135, 136, 159
Squire, 3, 5-7, 13, 14, 43, 44
Squire II, 9
Stephen, 52
Stonewall, 164
Suda M. Hemphill, 84, 106
Sue, 109
Susan, 140, 141
Susanna, 76
Susannah, 76, 77, 79, 117-119, 123, 159
Susannah (Nixon), 16, 43, 45, 71
Susannah M. , 79
Susannah Nixon, 44, 65, 71
Susie Evelyn, 99
Sylvanus Columbus, 116
T., 113
T.F., 127
Talmadge "Tab", 94
Taylor, 108, 109
Tempie Ann Harris, 83, 94
Tennie, 110
Terrissa/Tempie Ann, 136
Thelma Elizabeth, 91
Theodosia, 101
Thomas, 43, 45, 47, 75, 79, 81, 107, 115, 117, 123, 124, 127, 133, 159, 161, 169
Thomas "Big Tom", 139, 140, 142
Thomas Jr., 76, 77
Thomas Jr. , 79

       Thomas S., 139
       Thomas Samuel, 143
       Thomas Sr., 79
       Thomas W., 100, Addenda VII
       Thomas Wesley, 81, 83, 97
       Thomas Wiley, 113, 115
       Thomas "Big Tom", 139, 140
       Thomas, Sr., 79, 143
       Thos, 113
       Tillman, 86, 87, 93, 94, 127, 128, 132
       Tine, 166
       Tom, 99, 142
       Trissie, 87, 93, 127
       Trissie Malissa, 86, 93, 127
       W. Lawrence, 106
       Wallie R. , 99
       Willard, 168
       Willard H., 132
       Willard Kelse, 88, 91
       William, 69, 80, 140
       William D. , 101
       William Daniel, 27
       William H., 69, 165
       William Latimore, 134
       William McDuffy, 95
       William R., 113-115
       William Riley, 118, 121
       William Waightstall, 67, 69
       Willie Daniel "Bud, 99
       Woodard, 88
       Zebedee Vance, 105
       Zina, 168
       "Big Tom", 139
       "Little Tom", 124
Boone cemetery, 93, 127, 132, 139, 142
Boone Family Research Association, 49
Boone's Fork, 19, 43
Boonford, 132, 151, 161, 163, 164, 166
Bowlick
       Frances, 156

    James Martin, 155
    James Martin , 156
Bowman
    Lena Loretta, 141
Bradley
    Della, 96
    Jerry, 112
Branch
    John, 128
Braswell
    J.D., 158
Brittain Presbyterian Church Cemetery, 79
Broomer
    Margaret, 109
    Wil, 109
Brown
    Ambrose, 156
    Bernie, 156
    Frances Bowlick, 156
    George, 142
    Mabel, 156
Brum
    William, 109
Bryan
    Martha, 9
    Rebecca, 9
    settlement, 6
    William, 9, 43
Buchanan
    Sarah M., 132
    Sina, 132
    unknown, 158
Buckner
    Henry, 84
    Margaret, 108, 109
    Matilda Irene, 107, 108
    Sarahan, 109
Buna Vista, 163
Burleson
    Charles, 119

Burnett
> Nancy Jane, 38

Butner
> Henry, 103
> Sam, 142

Butt
> Robert, 101

Byler
> David, 39

Cabins in the Laurel, 128, 134, 167

Calloway
> Wm. Arsemus, 133

Camargo, Mexico, 162

Camp Jones, Va., 146

Camp Morton, 98

Campbell
> Frances Abigail, 95

Candler
> Naoma(Oma), 113

Cane River, 121, 163

Canipe
> Lula, 154

Cansler
> Eliza Anne, 24
> John, 27

Capps
> Sarah, 53

Carpenter
> Carolyn, 91

Carroll
> Mary, 141
> Noah, 127
> Sam, 132
> Vance, 94

Carter
> Mary, 9

Cassell
> Elizabeth, 3

Cates
> Gideon, 39

Chrisawn
- Thomas, 128, 134
- Vinnie, 130

Church
- Joe, 133

Clarke
- Alexander, 57
- Andrew, 60
- Clinton, 57
- Cornelius, 57
- Cornelius Wellington, 57, 58
- Cyrus Poore, 60
- David Porter, 59
- Eleanor Boone, 57
- Eveline Delia, 60
- Franklin Pierce, 59
- George Powell, 60
- George Rogers, 59
- Jehu, 57
- Jeremiah, 45, 57
- John Boone, 60
- John Hugh, 57
- Joseph Bogle, 58
- Julia Lucinda, 60
- Lee Murrell, 60
- Mary, 60
- Mary Eleanor, 59
- Nathan Lytle, 57, 59
- Nathan Lytle, Jr., 60
- Robert Burns, 59
- Samuel McAffee, 59
- Susan Minerva, 58, 60, 61
- Thomas D., 58
- William Boone, 58

Clements
- Cornelius, 80
- Margaret, 80

Cody
- Altha, 111

Coffey

A.M., 20
Anna, 19, 32
Anna Boone, 31
Asbury, 20, 39
Asbury Marvel, 39
Calvin, 32
Campbell, 40
Celia, 32, 33
Charlotte Caroline, 34
Daniel, 32
Daniel Boone, 32
Drury, 32
Elizabeth, 40
Elizabeth (Smith), 35
Emily, 32
family, 75
Finley Patterson, 34
Gilliam, 32
Hannah, 19
Hannah (Boone), 31
Hannah Boone, 35
Henry C., 33
Hezakiah, 33
Hodge R., 50
Irvin, 40
Isaac, 35
Israel, 33
J. Calvin, 33
James, 33
John Morgan, 35
Jonah, 33
Julia, 33
Lavinia, 40
Leland, 35
Martha E., 32
Marvel, 19-21
McCaleb, 33
Millie, 36
Milton, 33
Minerva Jane, 33

    Mira, 33
    Nathan, 36
    Rachel, 39
    Rachel Boone, 39
    Rebecca, 50
    Sally (Fields), 31
    Sarah (Sallie), 35
    Smith, 20, 21, 31, 35, 36
    Sophronia, 33
    Squire, 35, 40
    Temperance, 40
    Thomas, 31, 35
    Thomas Milton, 33
    unknown, 40
    Wellborn, 32, 33
    William, 20, 21, 31, 35
    William Brazeal, 40
    William Rufus, 33
    woman, 75
Coffey?
    Elizabeth, 45
Coffey's
    Gap, 19
Colder
    Herbert, 106
Cole
    Elizabeth, 84, 106
    Jim, 101
Coleman
    Nellie, 69
Collett
    Elizabeth, 33
    Harriett, 32
Company B of the 63rd Tennessee Regiment., 100
Conley
    Dock, 154
    Stonewall, 154
Cooper
    Capt. William, 50
    John, 50

Cordell
    Virginia Cynthia, 165
Cottrell
    Sarah (Sally), 32, 33, 34
County Gloucester, England, 4
Cove Creek , 146
Crawford
    Cordelia Edith, 108, 110
    David, 58, 61
    David, Jr., 61
Crissaun
    Grifen, 128
    Thomas B., 128
Cross
    Harriet Elizabeth, 60
Curtis
    Anna, 96
    Fred, 96
    Hezekiah, 32
    James, 95, 96
    Madge, 96
    Melvina Boone, 95
    Zeb, 96
Dale
    Laura, 94
Dans
    Earl, 99
Davis
    Lula, 140, 164, 168
Day
    Elizabeth, 35
    Myra, 35
    Sarah, 9
Dean
    Nell, 106
Delaney
    Laura, 136
Dempsey
    Nathan, 146
Detached Militia of NC, 45

Deyton
- Mary Jane, 118

Dinah, 20

Dixon
- J.L., 118, 119, 135

Dooley
- John Dale, 157

Draper
- manuscript, 14, 19

Edge
- Hannah, 105

Edmisten
- Abram (Abraham), 24

Edwards
- Alfred, 134

Elrod
- Alexander, 19

English
- Mary, 109

Estes
- Clarissa, 32
- Harriet, 66
- James Langston, 66
- John Boone, 66
- Langston Lorenzo, 66
- Madison, 66
- Madison Elija, 66
- Martha, 66
- Mary Elizabeth, 66
- Polly (Mary) Moore, 66
- Sallie, 35

Faragher
- John Mack, 14

Farthing
- Elizabeth, 59

Febuary
- Cassandra Melvina, 157
- Charlie Penderson, 156
- Dovie Vanella, 157
- Florence Virginia, 157

    Mordecai Frank, 155, 156
    Pansy Viola, 157
    Robert Jefferson, 157
    Ruby, 156
    William Isaac, 156
Fergerson
    Polly, 107
Fincannon
    George, 112
First Manassas, 169
Flemings Chapel Baptist Church, 56
Forbes
    Eliza, 151
    Emma, 151
    Ernest, 151
    Gladys, 151
    Hazel, 151
    L.H. "Doc", 151
    Marteen, 151
    Paul, 151
    William Maynard, 149, 150
Forney's Regiment , 967Fort Stedman, 132
Fortner
    Emma, 170
Foster
    R.Y., 151
Foulke
    Mary, 3
Fox
    George, 1
Gallaspy
    Asa, 60
Gallimore
    Ruby, 151
Gallos, Mexico, 162
Gamblin
    Thomas, 69
Gardner
    Ted, 99

Garland
> J. W., 82

Geisler
> Lula, 151

Gelette
> Julia Ann, 24

Gentry
> Bertha, 111

Geralds
> Sally Jackson, 53

Gibbs
> Tom, 105

Gragg
> Allen, 37, 38
> America, 37
> Celia, 19
> Celia Boone, 37
> Celia Caroline, 38
> Eliza, 37
> Elizabeth (Pulliam), 37
> Enoch, 37
> Isom, 37
> James Osmond, 38
> Jesse, 37
> John, 37
> John Shelby, 38
> Luzenia Emaline, 38
> Manerva Avaline, 38
> Mary Gilbert, 38
> Susan, 32
> William, 20, 37
> William (Buck), 21, 37
> William (Buck) II, 21
> William Alphonso, 38
> William I, 37
> William III, 37

Grant
> Elizabeth Boone, 14
> William, 9

Green

       Curtis, 154
       Martha Ann, 154
Green Lawn Cemetery, 98
Greene
       Mary, 32
       Susannah, 37
       unknown, 158
Griffith
       Anne, 3
Grigsby, 24
Grindstaff
       Henry, 161
       Virgie, 94
Groatiot Prison, 98
Gurley
       John W., 170
Guthrie
       Alma, 106
Haigler
       Millie, 28
Hale
       Myrtle, 101
Hall
       Cate, 148
       James A., 148
       John D., 147, 148
       John G., 148
       Ted, 150
Halyburton
       Mary Ann, 59
Hampton
       Dock, 100; Delilah, 148
Hardin
       John, 23
Hargrove
       Sidney, 105
Harrington
       Minnie, 151
Harris
       Amanda, 108

        Josie, 155
        Lewis, 37
        Minerva, 108
        Tempie Ann, 83, 94
        Thursey L., 108
        William, 108
Hartley
        Eliza, 58
        Levi, 57
Hayes
        unknown, 165
Hefiner
        Mrs. T.E., 84
Helton
        Judah, 24
Hemphill
        Suda M., 84
        Sarah Jane, 38
Henderson, 28
        Medie, 99
        Sarah, 19
Hensley
        Mack, 96
        W.J., 139
Hicks
        Jack, 147
        Kate, 94
Higgins
        J.W., 82
Hight
        Read, 27
Hinsley
        James H., Sr., 103
Hinson
        Charles Wright, 99
Hirton
        Sallie Emaline, 69
Hoilman
        Alice, 154
Hollifield

Hazel Webb, 151, 152, 173
Lillie, 134
Holmes
Emma, 165
Holt
Isabel, 63
Honeycutt
Emma, 102
Hopson
Molly, 154
Howell
Annie Mae ("Tine") , 166
Deborah, 3
Delilah, 77, 169
Dovie, 166; Frances, 155
James, 79, 161, Martha, 169
Naomi, 77, 161, 163, 164
Nayoma, 162
Ollie, 77, 146, 147
Oma, 163
Hughes
Columbus H., 149
David N., 87
Greenberry, 86, 87
Jeremiah, 140, 141
Louisa, 87
Maggie, 87
Martha Boone, 128
Mary Ann Laws, 87
Mary S. , 87
Minnie, 94
Robert, 87
Samuel, 87; Sarah J., 87, Sarena, 87
Thomas Greenberry, 141
William, 87
Zebulon , 87
Hughes Cemetery, 141
Huskins
Alexander, 86

    Alvin, 86
    Cleve, 86
    Ebbin, 86
    Ebbin E., 88, 89
    Rob, 86
    Thelma Elizabeth, 89
    Twin daughters, 86

Hutchins
    L. Belle, 139, 143

Hyatt Cemetery, 137

Hyde
    James M, 106

Jackson
    Sally, 53

Jenkins
    Ross, 151

Job Cemetery, 105

Johnson
    Tena Elizabeth, 105
    Yancey, 134

Johnston
    General, 147

Jones
    Cleveland, 154
    Frances Della, 60
    James, 94

Jopling
    Harriet Elizabeth, 67
    Mary Ann, 67

Jordan
    Julia Ann, 60

Julian
    Bertha Bell, 157
    Delilah Hampton, 148
    Eliza, 147-149, 155
    Elkanah "Cain", 155,157
     Cemetery, 147
    Flossie, 157
    James Norman, 148

Kalberlahn

Hans Martin, 14
Keith
- 2nd Lieutenant Alfred, 146
- Alfred, 145, 146
- Gen. A.F., 145
- General Alfred, 145

Kelley
- John B., 99

Kelsey Post Office, 19

Kincaid
- Isabella, 45, 56, 65
- James M. , 65
- John, 65
- Margaret (Dunn) , 65
- Robert, 65

Kincaid Cemetery, 44, 65

Kuhn
- Mary "Polly", 117

Lee
- Onie, 157

Lentz
- Wm., 148

Likens
- Susanna, 3

Lilly
- Peggy, 151

Linville
- Ann, 9

Littlejohn
- Mary Boone, 79
- Ann E., 68
- Azor, 67
- Azor Tillman, 55
- Daniel W. , 68
- Elijah Boone, 68
- Isabelle, 56
- John, 55, 56, 67
- John Boone, 56
- Margaret Emily, 68
- Martha, 56

    Martha L., 68
    Mary Boone, 55, 79
    Mary Isabelle, 56
    Mary Jane, 68
    Nancy Isabella, 68
    Sarah Boone, 67
    Sarah Frances, 56
    Susan, 56
    Thomas, 45, 55, 56, 68, 79
    W. Shuford, 56

Littlejohn Methodist Church , 56

Lost Cove, 146

Lower Creek Baptist Church, 59

Lunsford
    unknown, 165

Martin, 20

Mast, 37

Maugridge
    Mary Milton, 1

McAndrew
    Susan, 27

McCall
    Jacob M., 63
    John, 63

McCallister
    Elizabeth Hayes, 100
    Randolph, 100
    Rebecca Florence, 84, 100

McCourry
    Hannah, 132
    Martha, 127, 132
    Silas, 132

McCracken
    Willie, 94

McCurry
    Hattie Gribble, 155, 158

McDonald
    Elizabeth, 45, 51

McFarland
    Johnnie, 99

McGuire
    Polly, 36
McIntosh
    Mary, 84, 104
    unknown, 58, 61
McIntosh Cemetery, 75, 104
McIntyre
    Catherine, 106
McKinney
    James Preston, 157
McMahan
    Altha Jane, 86, 88, 89
    Barbara Blalock, 88
    Blanchey, 96
    Elendor/Nelly, 83, 85
    Elizabeth, 135, Addenda VI
    Jackson, 88
    James, 19
    John, 16
    John Sevier, 96
    Lucretia , 96
    Margaret, 77, 81, 96
    Mary, 81, 85, 87
    Mary Jane, 96
    Nancy C., 96
    Nelly, 84
    Riley, 96
    Riley A., 83
    Robert P., 96
    Sally, 77, 81, 83, 84
    Sarah, 16, 19, Addenda V
    Sarah Ann, 96, Sophronia, Addenda VI
    Thomas C., 96
    unknown, 85
    William Levi, 96
Medaris
    Hiram, 28
Medina Cemetery , 97
Melton
    Carrie, 60

    Ester, 88
    John, 83
Mexican War, 145, 146, 161, 163
    Co. K, 5th Regiment, Tennessee Volunteers, 146
    Company D, 1st North Carolina, 146
Miller
    Abraham Lincoln "Link", 157
    David, 165
Montgomery
    J.S., 99
Moody
    Elizabeth S. (Bowman), 55
Moore
    Betsy, 28
    Daniel, 27
    Elijah L., 32
    Elizabeth, 21
    Elizabeth Rebecca, 27
    Harriett, 33
    Jesse Richard, 34
    Judson, 37
    Martha, 69
    Martitia Emeline, 66
    Nancy, 35
    Polly, 32, 66
    Rachel, 66
    Rachel (Stone), 27
    Rufus Lafayette, 69
Morgan
    Edward, 5
    Sarah, 3
Morrow
    Elbert, 110
Moss
    David, 27
    Edward ("Neddie"), 24
    Neddie, 28
    William, 40
Mt. Pisgah United Methodist Church Cemetery, 108
Mulberry Watershed, 19

Murdock
    Florence, 165
NC Troops
    Company E, 136, 169
Neal
    James, 146
Nelson
    John H., 33
New River, 19
Nichols
    Nancy Miranda, 140, 142, 143
Nixon
    Susannah, 16
North Carolina Troops
    6th Regiment, 146
    6th Regiment, Co. E, 161, 169
    6th Regiment, Company E, 140
    Co. C, 16th North Carolina Regiment, 141
    Company B, 29th Regiment, 136
North Carolina Calvary
    Company B, 5th Battalion, 120
North Carolina Troops
    16th Regiment, 118
    16th Regiment, Co. B, 120
    Co. D., 29th Regiment, 121
    Company B, 54th Regiment, 132
    Company D, 29th Regiment, 120
North Carolina Troops
    Co. G, 50th Regiment, 80
    Company B, 29th Regiment, 98
    Company G, 50th Regiment, 80
North Cove Baptist Cemetery, 84
Norton
    Ann, 121
Oakes
    Isaac Douglas, 157
    Mabel Elizabeth, 156

Odle
    Mary ("Aunt Pop"), 45, 51

Ogle
    D.J., 99

Ollis
    Walter Brownlow, 157

Orr
    James, 40

Parks
    John Isham, 60

Parnell
    Charles, 1012Parrott
        Ann, 137
        Dolph, 137
        James, 137
        Lizzie, 101
        Sam, 101
        Samuel H., 136, 137
    Partin
        Lizzie, 96

Paterson's Unit, 146

Patty
    William, 40

Payne
    Col Robt, 162
    Henry Birtwell, 69

Penland
    Hettie, 88

Phillips
    James, 163
    James C. , 162

Pirtle
    Isaac Newland, 50

Plum Branch Baptist Church, 127

Plum Branch cemetery, 75, 93, 130

Poseley
    Ennie, 150

Powell
    Dewey, 149

    Emma, 58
    Evaline Delia, 57, 59
    George, 59
    Lucinda Rowe, 59
    Nettie, 95
Power   Bible, 43
    Eleanor Boone, 71
    John, 71
    John Jr., 16
Pritchard
    Isabelle Elizabeth, 150
Proctor
    Sam, 105
Puckett
    Martha Ann, 60
    Mrs. Emily, 57, 59
Puett
    William, 35
Quinton
    Willard J, 106
Quzsts
    Louisia (Harris), 83
Ramsey
    Anna, 102
    Ed Ramsey, 102
    Henry, 102
    Hiram, 102
    John, 84
    John C. , 102
    Kittie, 102
    Laura, 102
    Sallie, 102
    Thomas E., 102
    William C., 102
Randolph
    John, 100
    Sarah, 140
Ratliff
    Cora Lee, 154
    Jewell, 99

Ray
- Albert, 83
- Amos, 82
- Emily, 84, 104
- Jane, 118
- Joseph, 107
- Mexico, 124
- N.B. (Nate "Boone"), 119
- Thomas, 118
- William, 164
- William Billy, 118
- Willie, 140, 165

Rebel's Creek Cemetery, 165

Rich
- Mary ("Aunt Pop"), 51
- Mary "Aunt Pop", 45

Riddle
- George, 101

Roan Mountain, 146, 147

Robinson
- John C., 49
- Calvin, 170
- Florence, 170
- Jesse, 49
- Mira, 170
- Nettie, 170
- Wyatt, 170

Rountree
- unknown, 88, 91

Satillo, Mexico, 162

Schull's Mills, 19

Setzer
- Adam, 63, 65
- Jacob, 45, 63
- Jemima Boone, 63
- Mary Matilda, 65, 66
- Polly, 65

Shell
- John L., 149
- Emma, 59

Sheppard's
    Murial Early, 134
Shoemake
    Lulu Belle, 95
Silver
    David, 96;   Susan Alice, 116
    Delzie, 134;   Rachel, 127
    Frances (Frankie), 21
    Frankie, 65
    George, 95
Sims
    Sophia (Armstrong), 83
Sinclair
    Martha Patsy, 45, 71
    Thomas, 71
Snow Creek, NC, 163
Sparks
    Sarah, 164, 168
Spraker
    Hazel, 14
Standley
    Wiley, 36
Staton
    Fannie, 134
Steele
    John R., 59
Stephens
    Mary, 133
Stichcomb
    Dr. J. , 162
    Dr. John, 162
Stinchcomb
    Dr., 166
    Paul, 166
Stover
    Jacob, 3
Street
    Ed, 150
    Walter, 150
Surrell

Thomas, 26
Sutton
    Bud, 96
Swofford
    Elander, 84, 98
    James P., 84, 98
    John Henry, 84, 98; Sarah Ann, 84
    Zipporah, 84, 98
Synder
    Dudley, 151
Taff
    Minerva, 24
Taylor
    Benjamin Franklin, 56
    Dinah, 99
Terrell House Inn, 75, 104
Thomas
    James C., 141
    Marcus E., 132
Thomason
    Drucilla, 133
    Sarah Ann, 127
    Thomas J., 133
Three Forks Baptist Church, 19, 44
    Sarah Ann, 23
Thurman
    Juda M., 53
    Katherine, 53
Tipton
    Phoebe Naomi, 150
    Loretta Frances, 149
    Naomi, 149
Titanic, 167
Tolley
    Alice Whit, 156
    Alice Whit , 155
    Anna J, 158
    Clara Lee, 158
    Clyde A., 155
    Dock M., 155

    Edith, 158
    Elizabeth, 164
    Ethel, 158
    Frances Howell, 155
    Frank (Lunnie), 155
    George, 155, 158
    Georgia, 158
    Howard, 158
    James, 155
    John D., 147, 155
    John N. , 155
    Joseph, 155, 169
    Joseph Burl, 158
    Lillie M., 155
    Lillie N. , 157
    Maxine, 158
    Murl, 158
    Sarah Jane, 155-157
    Willa Jean , 158
    William, 155

Tom
    Mary Lou, 84

Triplett
    Emily, 27

Tritt
    John, 36

Tryon
    William, 6

Turbyfill
    Beatrice, 130

Tuttle
    Mary Elizabeth (Bettie), 34

Uppey
    Sarah, 1

VanCleve
    Jane, 9

Vickers
    Sarah Ann, 111
    Sarah Ann, 108

Wake Forest College, 59

Wallen
- J.W., 101

Walters
- Irene, 105

Ward
- Grover, 112

Wardrope
- Dorcas, 113

Warlick
- Elizabeth(Kincaid), 67

Warren
- Catherine Brown, 3

Washburn
- Nancy Caroline, 95

Webb
- Benjamin, 4
- Charlie Caleb, 154
- Ella, 35
- Eveline, 154
- Flora Pansy, 154
- George, 4
- Haska, 146
- James, 151
- James Washington, 147
- John, 1, 3-5
- Joseph, 4
- Landon, 154
- Liza Etta, 154
- Margaret LeGrand, 37
- Mary, 4
- Nathan Sylvester, 154
- Nathaniel, 154
- Obie, 154
- Sarah, 4
- Venna M., 154
- Washington Lee, 154

Webb
- John, Sr., 4
- Robert, 4

Westall

    Tom, 103
    Wm B., 79
Wilcoxen
    John, 5, 9
Williams
    Henrietta, 97
    Joe, 56
    Joseph Marion, 97
    Louise Ann, 105
    Pleasant Terry, 60
    Richard, 60
Willis
    Elizabeth (Bessie), 165, 166
    Landon, 96
    Mary Ann, 113, 115, 116
    Thomas, 110
    Wm., 162
Wilson
    Abner, 50
    Allen, 50
    Dr., 61
    Edward, 127
    Elizabeth, 50
    Hannah, 50
    Isaac, 162, 163
    Israel, 29
    James, 50
    Jesse, 45, 49, 164
    John, 50
    John Thomas, 70
    Jonathan, 19-21, 29, 50
    Levi, 29
    magistrate, 163
    Mary, 50
    Rachel Boone, 49
    Rachel Silver, 127
    Sarah, 77, 127
    Sarah Boone, 29
    Susannah, 50
    Tarlton, 49, 50

Woodfin, 100
    John S., 142
    W.C., 136
Yadkin Baptist Church, 43
York
    Martha, 108, 111
Yorktown, Virginia, 146, 147
Young
    George, 164
    Phagan McDaniel, 164
Zion Hill Baptist Church, 19
    Elizabeth, 27
    John, 23
    Jonathan, 39
Zion Hill Baptist Churchyard, 27

About the Author

Debra Webb Rogers, a former professional ballet dancer, graduated from Florida State University where she performed with their dance department while earning a B.S. degree in education.

She has been a company member with The Birmingham Ballet, The Israel Ballet, and The Florida Ballet. She has appeared in *Bride's* magazine and in a commercial that won both an Addy and an Emmy award.

She has written for the national magazine *Dancebag*, and is listed in *Who's Who Among America's Teachers*. She is currently on the faculty at Douglas Anderson School of the Arts in Jacksonville, Florida, where she was voted adjunct Teacher of the Year in 1997/98.

Thacker House Enterprises
Jacksonville, Florida
ISBN 978-0-9801919-0-5

Addenda 2011

This addendum contains more information on Jeremiah Boone (son of Thomas) and his descendants (see pg. 82). The information and photographs on the pages that follow were kindly provided by Patricia Robertson in June 2011.

Joe Farber Boone   b. 1907 ND   d. 1989 OR   mar. Cleo Marie Abbott

Participant #148385

Participant #149924

George Boone III   b. 1666 Eng.   d. 1744 PA   mar. Mary Maugridge

Squire Boone   b. 1696 Eng   d. 1765 NC   mar. Sarah Morgan

Israel Boone   b. 1726 PA   d. 1756 NC   mar. Unknown Wife's Name

Jonathan Boone   b. 1750 NC   d. 1826 NC   mar. Susanna Nixon

Thomas Boone   b. 1774 NC   d. 1855 NC   mar. Elizabeth W.

Jeremiah Boone   b. 1809 NC   d. 1899 NC   mar. Margaret McMahan

Mc Daniel S. Boone   b. 1845 NC   mar. Sophronia McMahan

Jerry W. Boone   b. abt 1869   d. 1952   mar. Alice Edge

Charles Edward Boone   b. 1908   d. 1978   mar. Ida M. Tyler

Participants father was born in Delaware less than 100 years ago.

Jeremiah Boone had the following children:
    (1st marriage)
    Robert Boone born about 1836.
    Caroline Boone
    Margaret Boone

    (2nd marriage)
    Thomas Wesley Boone born 1840.
    Baachus Boone born 1842 in Burnsville, N. C. and died March 1, 1８__
    (He was a volunteer in the Civil War.)
    Sarah Ann Boone born 1843 in Burnsville, N. C. and died about 1901
    McDaniel Boone born 1845.
    Edward A. Boone born 1846.
    Mary Jane Boone born 1847.
    Lucretia Boone born 1849.
    Jeremiah Sullins Boone born September 20, 1854.
    Ennis Clarke "Dove" Boone born March 15, 1854.
    Doctor Crumley Boone born 1859.

Jeremiah Boon (Thomas[5], Jonathan[4], Israel[3], Squire[2], George[1])

The Children of Jeremiah Boone (1802-Abt 1899) and (1st wife) Margaret McMahan (1802-1840)			
Name	Birth	Death	Marriage
James E. Boon	1831	1861	
Robert Boon	1834		
Caroline Boon	1835		
Margaret Boon	1840		

The Children of Jeremiah Boone (1802-1885?) and (2nd wife) Sallie McMahan (1828-1861)			
Name	Birth	Death	Marriage
Thomas Wesley Boon	1840	1919	
Baachus Boon	1842	1864	
Sarah Ann Boon	1843	1901	
McDaniel S. Boon	1845		
Edward Boon	1846	1904	
Mary Jane Boon	1847	1935	
Lucretia Boon	1849	1935	
Jeremiah Sullins Boon	1854	1932	
Ennis Clark Dove Boon	1858	1939	
Doctor Crumbly Boon	1859	1933	

In the photograph below, Jeremiah's wife is probably incorrectly identified as Margaret. The picture is more likely of his second wife, Sallie. Margaret was born in 1802 and died in 1840. She married Jeremiah in 1826. Her sister Sarah (Sallie) McMahan was born 1828 and died in 1861. She married Jeremiah in 1839.

Jeremiah Boone (1802 – January 1885) son of Thomas Boone, with his wife Margaret McMahan. Photo taken about 1850.

Edward A. Boone, son of Jeremiah Boone and Grandson of Thomas Boone. Photo taken about 1867

Mary Jane Boone (seated) daughter of Jeremiah Boone with other unidentified ladies of Burnsville Yancey Co. N.C. Photo taken about 1903

Thomas Boone (22 April 1848 – 21 January 1921) son of Samuel Boone and grandson of Thomas Boone. of Yancey County, N.C.. Photo taken about 1878.

McDaniel Boon

(Jeremiah^6, Thomas^5, Jonathan^4, Israel^3, Squire^2, George^1)

The Children of McDaniel S. Boon (1845-?) and Sophronia McMahan Boon (1847-?)			
Name	Birth	Death	Marriage
Mary E. Boon	1867		
Jerry Washington Boon	1869	1952	
Julie J. Boon	1869 (twin of Jerry?)		
Hattie E. Boon	1873		
Thomas Walter Boon	1875	1941	
Charlie L. Boon	1881		
Doctor Crumbly Boon	1886	1939	

Sophronia McMahan Boon was the daughter of George W. Boon (1815-1868, son of Thomas Boone), and Elizabeth McMahan (1827-1870).

McDaniel (Little Mack) Boone   Sophronia McMannan Boone
Parents of J.W. Boone

This is a photograph of McDaniel Boone (Father) (Little Mack) and his sons. From left to right are:

McDaniel Boon; Charles Boon (1881-); Jerry Washington (J.W. or Bud) Boon (1869-1952); Thomas Walter Boon (1875-1941); Doctor Crumley (Crum) Boon (1886-1939); Don (Daniel) Boon (1884-).

McDaniel's firsborn was a daughter: Mary E. Boon ((1867-)
                                      Julie J. Boon (1869-)
                                      Hattie E. Boon (1873-)

Civil War Record of McDaniel Boon

U.S. Civil War Soldier Records and Profiles - Ancestry.com

Return to McDaniel S Boone

Compare With People From Your Family Tree

Children (4):
- Jerry Washington "Bud" Boone
- Hattie E. Boone
- Thomas Walter Boone
- Charlie I. Boone

McDaniel S Boone
B: Apr 1844 in Boones Ridge, Yancey, North Carolina, USA
D: , Yancey, North Carolina, USA

Parents:
Jeremiah Boon (1809-1865)
Sarah Sallie McMahan (1810-1894)

Sophronia Boone

U.S. Civil War Soldier Records and Profiles

Name:	**McDaniel Boone**
Enlistment Date:	15 Apr 1863
Rank at enlistment:	Private
Enlistment Place:	Buncombe County, NC
State Served:	North Carolina
Service Record:	Enlisted in Company K, North Carolina 7th Cavalry Regiment on 15 Apr 1863.
Sources:	North Carolina Troops 1861-65, A Roster

Source Information:
Historical Data Systems, comp. U.S. Civil War Soldier Records and Profiles [database on-line].

Jerry Washington Boon
(McDaniel[7], Jeremiah[6], Thomas[5], Jonathan[4], Israel[3], Squire[2], George[1])

J.W. Boon

Alice Boon, wife of J.W. Boon

The Children of Jerry Washington Boone (1869-1952) and Alice Mary Edge (Abt.1867-1932)			
Name	Birth	Death	Marriage
William "Willie" "Bill" Boon	1898		
Hannah Boon	1900 (triplet)	1967	
Daniel E. Boon	1900 (triplet)	1938	
Henry H. Boon	1900 (triplet)		
Hattie Tom Boon	1903	1938	
Frank Edward Boon	1907 (twin)	1956	
James Zebulon Boon	1907 (twin)	1965	
Charlie Boon	1908	1978	

THE STORY OF OUR BOONE HERITAGE

Tenth Generation

Jerry Washington (Bud) Boone

Jerry (Bud) Washington Boone

Jerry Washington Boone was born January 13, 1869 in Yancey County, North Carolina. He married Mary Alice Edge daughter of Jason Edge and Mary Boone Edge. Alice was born May 25, 1868 in Yancey County, North Carolina. He and his wife lived for some time in Madison County, North Carolina. They moved to Marion, McDowell County, North Carolina. Jerry was a blacksmith like his father.

Rev. Charles Boone recalls a humorous incident when his grandfather was living with them. His grandfather had gone to the doctor and he had prescribed a large bottle of medicine. It was on the mantle shelf of the fireplace. His grandfather picked up the bottle of medicine, turned it up and drank it all then with a big sigh replied, that "Dr. Haggnumum (Haggna) is a mighty good doctor". Alice Edge Boone died September 22, 1932 at the age of 64, and

My Grandpaw

Charles Boon

(Jerry Washington[8], McDaniel[7], Jeremiah[6], Thomas[5], Jonathan[4], Israel[3], Squire[2], George[1])

The Children of Charles Boone (1908-1978) and Ida M. Tyler (1908-1975)			
Name	Birth	Death	Marriage
Alice May Boone	1934		
Henry Alvin Boone	1936	2006	
Thomas Norwood Boone	1938	1986	
Charles Howard Boone	1941	2000	
Patricia Ann Boone	1944		
Sandra Lee Davis	1953		

Charles Boon

Charlie Boone   1908 – 1978
Blacksmith

My father was born on February 27th, 1908 to Jerry Washington and Alice Boone in Madison County, North Carolina, and grew up in the area known as the Toe River Valley. He was the youngest of their eight children and became a man of many talents as did most of the Boones from his branch. An accomplished Blacksmith, (passed on from his ancestors in England), a talented musician of many instruments, (his favorite being the piano) and he was an expert woodsman and a crack shot, a must to survive in the mountains at that time.

Most of the Boones from that part of the Blue Ridge Mountains were descendants of Israel Boone, oldest son of Squire Boone and older brother of the great frontiersman Daniel Boone who settled in that part of the country before moving on into Kentucky and Missouri. Blacksmithing, hunting, making music and whisky was part of their culture and none doubted that Jesus Christ was the Son of God. They did not run from trouble and tried to avoid it, however, trouble somehow had a way of finding many of them.

As a young boy his older brothers would take him along with them on their journeys and taught him the art of "riding the rails" and the necessity of being on the look out for the "bulls" of the railroad along the way. This knowledge learned at a young age became a priceless lesson later in his life. His formal education as he tells us lasted only until the third grade, long enough to learn the beautiful penmanship we all envied.

About 1931 or 1932, at a work camp in Tennessee, he and is brother James (they called him Buck) got into a scrap with two other young men, drinking was involved, bragging and provoking and of course someone pulled a knife. After the smoke settled a man lay dying on the floor. Everyone knew the

Boone brothers, they'd all sang and danced to Charlie's music and knew them well and where they were from. Frightened the two brothers ran away and left the area. They split up and each went in a different direction. My father became Edward Davis and eventually settled in Delaware. My uncle Buck became Charlie Howard and settled in Ohio.

It was "the Depression" and "riding the rails" was the only way to get from place to place. Trains were a sure fire way to get somewhere else fast and be out of sight at the same time. During this time in my father's life he developed his love of the trains. He became aquainted with how they were built, what made them run, the signals and where they went and what time.

When he married my mother she was not aware of his past until their first child was over a year old. She thought she married Edward Davis from Ashland, Kentucky. They had six children born "Davis," but as children we were all told "the story" and grew up knowing that was not actually our "real name." We all loved our father and knew the truth that's all that mattered. He made his living as a machinist and maintenance mechanic but there was always an anvil in the shed.

As children we did not get our toys from Montgomery Ward or Sears Robuck, our swing set, wagon, scooter and see-saw were made of metals and welded together by his hands, even some of my mothers pots and pans.

During the early 1950's he began his first scale model train, "the New York Central," a "stream liner." Then it was "the Great Northern," He made another "smoke stack steamer" but I do not know her name. He made all the parts in detail and cast them by hand.

The Civil War Centennial was approaching and "the Great Locomotive Chase" starring Fess Parker was playing at the Warner Theatre in Wilmington and I had been to see it. I came home all excited about the movie and simply said to him, "daddy, will you make the General for me?" I Loved the cow catcher, the smoke stack and the bell on top. He said, "I'll think about it." It was finished in the summer of 1960 and took him about a year. I was 16 years old and it has been in my possession ever since.

It was about 1965 when we entered the trains and many other tools and artifacts he had made in a craft show and again in the early 70's at the Delaware State Fare in Harrington in the senior division. Each time winning the blue ribbon. Many folks thought the trains were from a kit. All together he made four scale model trains.

Charles Boone (Edward Davis) died in 1978 always missing his mountains. In 2009 my nephew Danny, son of my deceased brother Charles Howard Davis, had his DNA tested through "the Boone Society" DNA testing program to prove our lineage as we knew it. The gene can only be passed from father to son. Of course the test came back a positive match and is recorded on their DNA project web site.

Some say the skill of the Blacksmith is genetic, passed from father to son, a talent from God. I believe that to be true.

Patricia Robertson   March 28, 2010
(Patsy Boone)

Charlie Boone

James (Buck) Boone

Charlies son:
Howard
daughter Alice
daughter Patsy
about 1948/49

Charlie Davis Boon and Ida

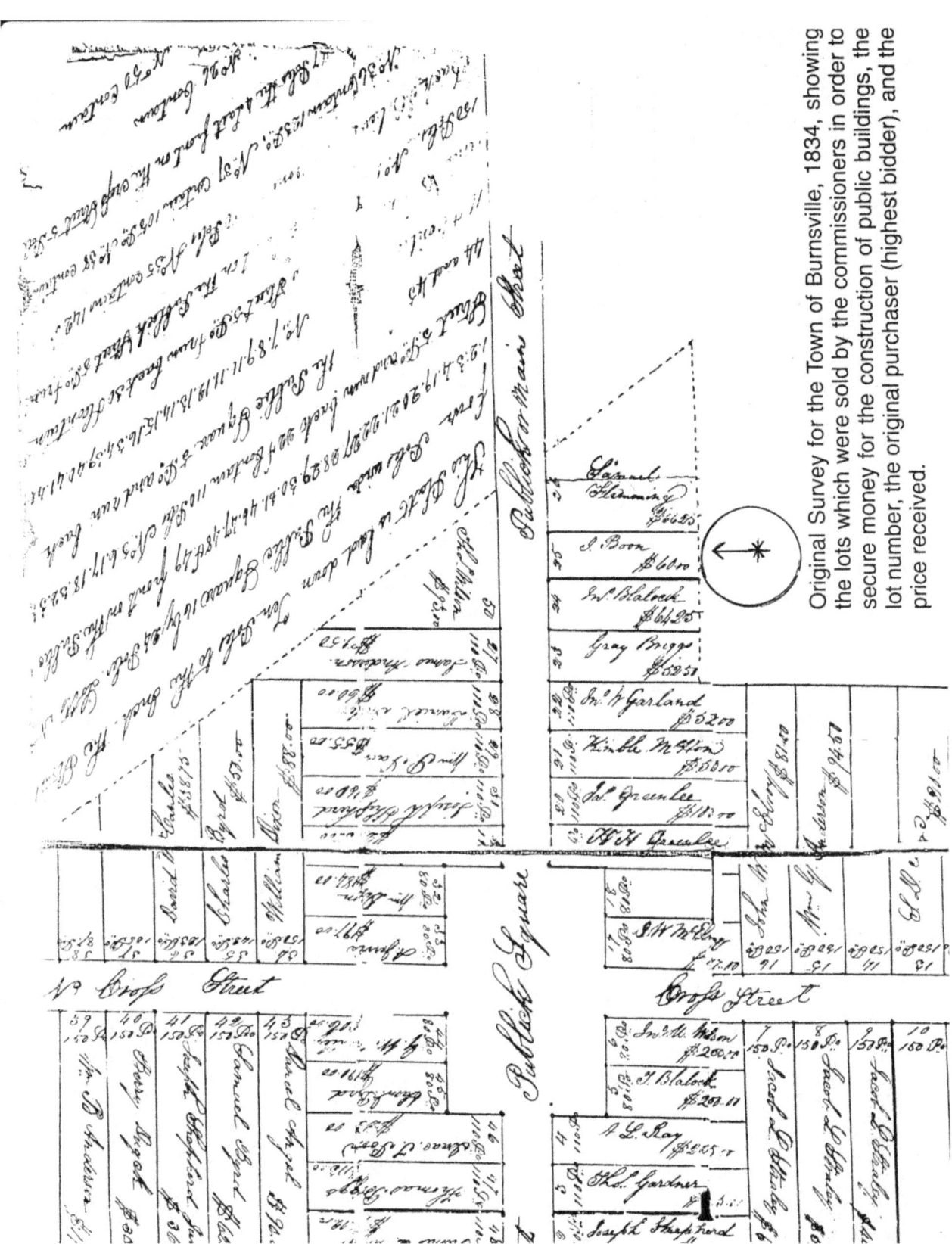

Original Survey for the Town of Burnsville, 1834, showing the lots which were sold by the commissioners in order to secure money for the construction of public buildings, the lot number, the original purchaser (highest bidder), and the price received.

www.ingramcontent.com/pod-product-compliance
Lightning Source LLC
Chambersburg PA
CBHW080430230426
43662CB00015B/2232